TOURISM: LEISURE AND RECREATION

TOURISM: LEISURE AND RECREATION

(In 3 Volumes)

(Tourism and Resource Management)
Volume 2

Editor
Sanchey Malviya

ISHA

ISHA BOOKS
Delhi-110033

Tourism: Leisure and Recreation
(Tourism and Resource Management)

Rs. 2500 (Set)
Rs. 835 (Each Volume)

ISBN : 81-8205-213-0 (Set)
ISBN : 81-8205-314-5 (Vol. 2)

Published in 2005 in India by
Isha Books
D-43, Prithviraj Road,
Adarsh Nagar, Delhi - 110033
e-mail : ishabooks@hotmail.com

Laser Typesetting at : Global Printers, New Delhi
Printed at :
Rajdhani Printers, Ph. : 011-23215190

Contents

Preface

Tourism is the act of travel for the purpose of leisure, recreation, and the provision of services for this act. It is one of the world's largest industries and one of its fastest growing economic sectors. Many sovereignties, along with their respective countries and states, depend heavily upon travel expenditures by foreigners as a source of taxation and income for the enterprises that sell services to these travellers. Consequently the development of tourism is often a strategy employed either by a non-governmental organisation or a governmental agency to promote a particular region for the purpose of increasing commerce through exporting goods and services to non-locals.

Written for the use of students, researchers, professionals and policy planners in the field of tourism, the present publication elaborately narrates the major issues and concerns in this rapidly growing field. The first volume, *Tourism: Policies, Planning and Governance* is concerned with the planning and governance of tourism. The second volume, *Tourism, Environment and the Society* discusses the environmental and social impacts of tourism in detail. The third volume, *Tourism and Resource Management* describes various strategies to effectively manage tourism and its resources. This highly informative, authentic and up-to-date work will be interesting to all those concerned with tourism, leisure and recreation.

Editor

1

Tourism: Issues and Opportunities

Tourism is the world's largest industry and studies predict its increasing growth. At the international level, tourism has traditionally been measured in international tourist arrivals and international tourist receipts. The World Tourism Organization (WTO) estimates that between 1950 and 1999, the number of international arrivals has grown from 25 million to 664 million, corresponding to an average annual growth rate of 7%. Receipts from international tourism (excluding international fare receipts) rose by an estimated 3.1% in 1999 to reach US$455 billion. This translates into an average receipt of US$685 per arrival. In addition, domestic tourism is of major importance in many countries.

Tourism creates jobs and contributes over 10% Gross Domestic Product (GDP), as well as brings in capital investment and exports. Socially and culturally, tourism offers the opportunity of providing jobs for minority and disadvantaged groups, creating adequate training in management skills, education and technology to local people and increasing incomes in rural and local economies, thereby contributing to the alleviation of poverty in developing countries. Environmentally, it is essential for tourism to maintain an optimal balance of its natural resources to ensure the ongoing arrival of tourists to destinations.

As the fastest growing and one of the most profitable industries in the world, tourism offers unparalleled opportunities for the economic development of local communities. Where traditional economic activities are in decline, employment in tourism related activities can offer many new opportunities. Properly managed tourism development can help to stem the out-migration of youth and other marginally-employed members of the community, alleviate poverty by providing new employment opportunities, revitalise traditional building and craft industries, enhance both the physical and the intangible heritage and offer a positive, peaceful way for communities to express pride in their cultural identity.

Painful experience in many areas of the world however, has shown that unplanned tourism development, although it may be profitable in the short term, can do irreversible damage to humankind's most precious heritage sites. Tourism can undermine the heritage value of these sites, despoiling them for future generations of inhabitants, students and visitors. The tourism juggernaut has the power to destroy the landscape with inappropriate infrastructure, force the out-migration of indigenous populations and cause over-exploitation and deterioration of the fragile cultural and natural resources. This vicious downward spiral also undermines heritage tourism by degrading and devaluing the very resources on which the tourism is based.

In historic towns and cities, where living traditional ways of life are threatened by tourism development driven by forces external to the community, local inhabitants can easily become side-lined from the benefits of tourism development. In addition, municipal government budgets and local taxpayers are unfairly burdened where the increased costs of site maintenance are not being compensated by increased revenues from the tourist industry, who are ultimately the users and consumers of the heritage.

The challenge is to move from the existing ad hoc approach, to one that can integrate the current social, economic and environmental programmes, funds and initiatives, and evolve new patterns of managing tourism businesses in a more systematic and dynamic way.The inevitable transition to sustainable development strategies gives the tourism industry an opportunity to confirm itself as a solution, rather than a contributor to the economical, social and environmental challenges facing the future.

One of the main barriers to achieving this goal in the past has been the inherent fragmentation of the industry, and the relative fragility of viable operating margins, especially for the small and medium-sized enterprises that make up most of the industry.This has indirectly led to a deficiency of accountability both by the private and public sectors.This lack of responsibility towards tourism is leading, at an ever-increasing rate, to an eventual environmental, economic and cultural crisis. In order to avert this crisis all stakeholders including, the public and private sectors, NGOs, trade unions and consumers need to begin to co-operate to make tourism work for everyone.

The way forward for tourism is to create strong partnerships between the private and public sectors, NGOs, institutional bodies, and local communities, in order to ensure effective active participation by all stakeholders. Governments are only just beginning to take a more decisive role in developing sustainable, economically successful tourism. But, strong partnerships by all players will bring valuable networking processes, workable policies and logical planning and development, transforming tourism's sometimes negative environmental image to one of sustainability and stewardship.

In 1992 at the Rio Earth Summit, 178 governments approved Agenda 21 and the Rio Declaration. Agenda 21 offered a blueprint for sustainable development, while the Rio Declaration articulated the main principles for sustainable development in the 21st century. Both documents challenged organisations, governments and industries to work towards maximum levels of sustainability, defined by the Brundtland Commission in 1987 as 'development that meets the needs of the present without compromising the ability of future generations to meet their own needs'.

Since the summit, the social, political and economic world has developed at a rapid pace.The encroaching globalisation of the world, the increasing necessity and use of technology, and its inherent liberalisation, have altered the way business is conducted and in so doing have affected the relationships between people and the environment. The inevitable global shift towards 'globalisation' is transforming the workplace, the job market, lifestyles, communities, industries and markets.

The challenge for stakeholders involved in all industries is to find a balance between sustenance, prosperity and people's desire to improve their financial/ material well-being, with the underlying need for identity, community, religion, home and family.Tourism can play a vital role in balancing these forces. It not only provides the livelihoods for both rural and urban communities, but has the capacity, when planned, developed and managed properly, to enhance community relations and build bridges of understanding and peace between nations.

Tourism also plays a crucial role in encouraging governments to reduce their barriers to growth.Thomas Friedman in his book The Lexus and the Olive Tree suggests that governments need to don a 'golden straight jacket' in order to allow pure free market capitalism and enable both developed and developing countries to achieve full economic growth within a sustainable development framework.

The first step to achieving this balance between sustainable development and economic growth for tourism was in 1996.The World Travel & Tourism Council (WTTC), the World Tourism Organisation (WTO/OMT) and the Earth Council, together launched *Agenda 21 for the Travel & Tourism Industry:Towards Environmentally Sustainable Development* - a sectoral action plan for sustainable development based on the outcome of the Rio Earth Summit in 1992. At the time it was the only industry-specific adaptation of Agenda 21.

The following definition of tourism was officially adopted by the United Nations Statistical Commission in 1993: 'Tourism comprises the activities of persons travelling to and staying in places outside their usual environment for not more than one consecutive year for leisure, business and other purposes'. Both the inter-governmental WTO/OMT and the private sector WTTC consider the tourism sector to be one of the largest - if not THE largest - in the world, particularly in terms of its contribution to the world economy.

According to WTTC estimates, tourism achieved the following economic impact directly and indirectly in 2001:

— USD3.3 trillion contribution to global GDP, almost 11% of total GDP;

— 207 million jobs worldwide, over 8% of all jobs;

— USD630 billion in capital investment, almost 9% of all capital investment.

This economic activity of the tourism sector was generated by 698 million international tourist arrivals in 2000, representing an estimated 7.3% increase over 1999 according to preliminary estimates.This was the highest growth rate in nearly a decade and almost double the increase of 1999 with nearly 50 million more arrivals recorded, which is approximately what destinations such as Spain or the United States receive in the entire year. In less than a decade, international tourist arrivals are projected to reach one billion.

In March 2001,WTO/OMT submitted a concise report on Sustainable Development of Tourism to the United Nations (UN), in which it noted that 'the development of tourism has been characterised by continuing geographical spread and diversification of tourist destinations. While in 1950 the top 15 tourist destinations, all in western Europe and North America, attracted 97% of the world's total arrivals, by 1999 this figure had fallen to 62%, with market shares increasing for developing countries and economies in transition, particularly in south-east Asia, central and eastern Europe, and Latin America.' The report also noted some of the main qualitative trends seen in the industry in the form of increased market segmentation, the development of new forms of tourism - especially those related to nature and wildlife, rural areas and culture - and how such programmes are influencing traditional package tours.

Clearly, tourists are increasingly selective about destinations and are demanding higher quality products and services. One of the driving forces behind this trend is the emergence of an 'experience-based economy', a term used by B Joseph Pine and James H Gilmore in the

Harvard Business Review, to describe what happens when 'a company intentionally uses services as the stage, and goods as props, to engage individual customers in a way that creates memorable events'. The tourism industry simultaneously thrives upon this trend and is threatened by it. Tourism products and services that demonstrate 'greater sensitivity to the environment, traditional culture and local people at the destinations' can create such an experience, whereas tourism in a context of uncontrolled growth which puts increasing pressure on the natural, cultural and socioeconomic environment, risks diminishing the visitor's experience. In short, increased market demand for experiences can contribute to social, economic and environmental sustainability only if the resulting pressures from growth are properly planned and managed.

The tourism industry is both receptive and conscious of the resulting pressures from economic growth and the need to protect our natural and social environment.The preservation of the tourism product - the environmental, social or cultural heritage specific to each country - is the only way to ensure a future for everyone. In response to this increase in recognition of the need to safeguard natural resources, a growing number of tourism companies are seeking to create more responsible consumer behaviour by using their products and services to educate and inform their customers. Many multinational companies have all adopted 'corporate citizenship' programmes that have created dialogue between the community and the private sector, as well as promoting sustainable development.

Economic Impacts

Tourism, if utilised effectively, can be a force for positive growth and economic success for both developed and developing countries. Markets have the potential to enhance lives in a sustainable framework through providing wealth creation, choice, innovation and competition. The tourism industry contains these four elements that enable it to be a dynamic market force for sustainability in the future. It has the capacity to increase exports, bring in capital investment, boost an economies GDP and create employment.

Tourism generates jobs throughout the economy, both in companies directly involved in the business and in related supplier industries such as retail, construction, manufacturing and telecommunications. WTTC estimated that tourism generated 203 million jobs - over 8% of all jobs worldwide - in 2000, rising to over 207 million in 2001. Within a decade, this is estimated to increase to over 260 million jobs or 9% of all employment.These jobs employ a significant proportion of women, minorities and young people and are predominantly in small and medium-sized enterprises (SMEs).

SMEs make up the majority of the tourism sector, although the exact percentage is unknown. SMEs encourage entrepreneurs, provide many diverse job opportunities and enable low skills entry for emerging countries. Successful human resource management, in the shape of training and education, is crucial to achieve the economic prosperity, for both SMEs and the larger multinational companies that can be accrued through tourism.

Highly competitive destinations are realising that quality of services and facilities are vital to ensure a consistency of tourists to the destination. On the other hand the fragmentation of the industry and the high proportion of SMEs has led to unconstructive training and protection for employees. Given the number of low-skilled workers in the sector, the industry has been criticised for offering nothing more than 'hamburger flipping' jobs that contribute little to the sustainability of an economy or society.

The tourism industry is renowned for its high turnover, anti-social working hours, low pay, seasonal employment, instability and low job status. However, this does not tell the whole story. Jobs for the Millennium - Mexico, a report produced in 2000 by the WTTC and the Fundacitón Pro-Educación en Turismo, AC (FUTUR), paints a different picture of the hospitality workforce. While over 36% of the employees in over 200 companies surveyed were considered 'unskilled', almost a quarter of the jobs at these companies required professional or managerial competence, and over 45% required some level of skill.

Despite SMEs offering their employees transferable skills, there is still a considerable absence of training for these groups.There is a real need for human resource development within the sector that tackles the issues that lead to costly effects for tourism. Indeed, more than a third of employers surveyed reported serious shortages of skilled workers, which would suggest that real career opportunities do exist.This has met with industry recognition of the need for human resource development that raises the industry's profile, increases productivity and provides sustainable employment.

One of the catalysts creating the urgency for trained, skilled workers within the industry is the increasing use of information technology. Tourism is reliant on a human service, yet is increasingly using technology to facilitate the sector in competitive pricing.The growth in tourism forecast for the next ten years, will lead to a greater dependency on information technology, which will become more important in the future as the industry copes with rapid expansion and sophistication of the tourism and hospitality supply.

In order to achieve sustainable economic growth, the tourism sector needs to reduce social, economic, environmental and cultural barriers. Some of the major obstacles to this growth are the lack of infrastructure, environmental degradation and fragile linkages that weaken a country's tourism potential. One way to address these barriers is for the sector to foster tourism investment through public-private sector partnerships that not only enable a country to grow economically, but retain the essential social, cultural and environmental assets that make each country a unique product.

Public-private sector co-operation and planning are also essential to creating sustainable employment in the tourism industry, and to this end the private sector has fought for recognition of its true contribution to job growth and economic development. Hitherto, the industry had been disadvantaged by a lack of data reflecting its full economic impact. Only recently has the methodology known as Tourism Satellite Accounting (TSA), pioneered by WTTC,WTO/OMT and others, been developed and accepted by governments as a means for fully measuring tourism's contribution as an economic activity. TSA is based on a 'demand-side' concept of economic activity (i.e. the economic activities of visitors and travel companies), as tourism does not supply a homogenous product or service.

Unlike traditional industries (agriculture, electronics, steel, etc.), tourism is a diverse set of industries offering a multitude of products (consumer and capital durables and non-durables), and services ranging from airline and cruise ship fares and accommodations, to restaurant meals, entertainment, souvenirs and gifts, immigration and park services, recreational vehicles and automobiles, aircraft manufacturing and resort development.

By using input/output modelling,TSA is able to differentiate between tourism industry supply and economy supply, including that portion of supply which it imports from abroad. Additionally, it breaks down the supply side accounts into direct and indirect impacts and the individual elements of GDP (wages and salaries, transaction taxes, operating surplus, depreciation and subsidies).These data ensure governments have a broader understanding of the impact of tourism, in particular the implications of policy for the tourism economy.

TSA data also reiterates the fact that tourism has the potential to be a catalyst industry for emerging countries to kick-start their economies, offering many opportunities that are not available in other industries. For example, the rise in cultural, heritage and wildlife niche market tourism, in developing countries, is becoming a viable alternative for communities that want to move away from mono-culture farming, which can not only destroy sustainable patterns of agriculture and traditional fertility cycles but has been associated with negative changes in social structures and economic relationships. Annual research undertaken by WTTC demonstrates that the impact of tourism on the whole economy is much greater than the size of the industry itself. For every dollar spent on tourism, a further dollar and a half is typically contributed to GDP in other sectors of the economy.

Social Impacts

Tourism can be both a force for the preservation of or, conversely, a threat to a community's natural and cultural heritage.A 1999 report Sustainable Tourism and Cultural Heritage published by the World Bank underscores the symbiotic nature of the relationship.The mutual dependence that exists between tourism and cultural heritage is becoming more evident. While culture heritage creates a foundation for tourism's growth, tourism has the power to generate funds that make conservation possible.

Cultural heritage loses much of its meaning without an audience, and a society participating in and benefiting from it. Without sustainable management, tourism loses its potential for growth. With the growing interest in culture and community, tourism is finally being recognised as an industry that can boost rural economies, create entrepreneurs and jobs and help preserve indigenous cultures.

Above all, tourism offers a better life not just for those who make money, but for those who pay money to enjoy it. For example, trekking tourism has led to the transformation of the traditional subsistence farming of the Sherpas of the Khumbu region into a cash economy that has generated income, jobs and a better standard of living.

One of the main challenges, therefore, for all stakeholders involved in tourism, including local authorities, NGOs and businesses, is to maintain an optimal balance to ensure sustainability. Otherwise, in destinations where the natural and cultural heritage deteriorates, the economy will be put at risk as tourists migrate to better-preserved destinations.

The Addo Elephant National Park in South Africa's Eastern Cape Province aimed to integrate community tourism initiatives with mainstream tourism. A multi-stakeholder dialogue process was adopted including all private and public sector voices.The outcome was that local groups have the potential to add diversification to a primarily wildlife destination and the private sector has the key for effective marketing and business development skills.

Research suggests that following the trends already mainstream in other economic sectors, social responsibility and corporate citizenship are expected to become in the future issues of strong concern requiring a response from the tourism industry as a whole, as well as at corporate level.The concept of 'corporate citizenship' is now being adopted by many of the key leaders in the private sector of tourism and is emerging as a central issue for business companies.

Corporate citizenship recognises the need to create a balance between all stakeholders' needs, society's different interests and the sustainability of the natural environment with a greater focus on governance and accountability. It is about taking responsibility for, and doing as well as possible in terms of social, environmental and economic performance given competitive opportunities and constraints.The business case and corporate citizenship have become joined in current debate about the changing role of business in society.

The Award for Responsible Capitalism 2001 - sponsored by First Magazine- was presented to Marilyn Carlson Nelson, chair and CEO, Carlson Companies and highlights the importance of corporate citizenship for multinationals. Profit can serve many functions, and within tourism modern business leaders are using it for good purposes. Multinationals can help contribute to the wealth and welfare of us all, and increasingly leading players in the tourism industry are recognising the importance of the contributions they can make to the communities within which they work.

Corporate citizenship balances the interests of the economy with those of public policymakers, individuals and groups in civil society. It can not only improve the quality of life for distressed communities, but can also generate tangible returns for the bottom line. Within tourism, corporate citizenship is becoming an increasingly important concept for the private sector.

Environmental Impacts

The tourism industry has come far since the Earth Summit in Rio de Janeiro, in 1992, when the impact of industries on the environment was high on the political agenda. The increasing numbers of travellers and the rise in package tours during the 1980s were causing a valid concern among environmentalists.

WTTC, with WTO/OMT and the Earth Council, in response to the scrutiny with which tourism was judged, collaborated and produced Agenda 21 for the Travel & Tourism Industry.This public-private sector effort was designed to ensure that as tourism grew globally, its influence would not have an undesirable impact on the environment. Indeed all areas of tourism have over the last decade implemented many individual environmental schemes and programmes, not for-profit funds and foundations all over the world.

Recently there has also been an increase in conferences on the environment hosted by governments and by private sector companies, which are highlighting the responsibility of both the public and private sector to protect natural and cultural heritage and emphasise the importance of environmental sustainability. If tourism is not planned and managed carefully, it can overwhelm the very assets with which it attracts visitors to the destination. Examples of tourism expansion, that have ignored the local environment, are well-known:

— tourism facilities built on pristine land without prior consultation with the local community;

— golf greens that use up scarce water supplies;

— water pipes and infrastructure that feed major developments but often ignore the local village.

With the rise of mass tourism comes the threat of destruction of fragile eco-systems and coastal regions, local culture, and the depletion of natural resources. Conversely, tourism can generate the necessary revenue to protect and preserve biodiversity and act as a force for environmental protection especially in developing countries. Game parks and nature preserves are centres of institutional strength and can act as a focus for tourism development in rural areas.

Tourism helps generate resources to maintain these protected areas, as illustrated by the Royal Chitwan National Park in Nepal, the Masai Mara in Kenya and the rainforests of Costa Rica. Not only can it help to preserve the environment, but profits have a greater potential to reach local and rural communities, compared to other sectors.

The new concept of eco-tourism or nature tourism is experiencing faster-than-average growth. Eco-tourism alone contributed $154 billion in receipts in 2000 and is growing 20% annually compared with just 7% for tourism overall in an already booming industry, and reflects those consumers who are aware of the issues facing tourism.

There are indications that consumers are also beginning to influence businesses, as they become more aware of the choices available to them, and of this rapid growth in the ecotourism niche market. However, eco-tourism alone is not the answer to addressing the environmental problems facing the industry. It also remains to be seen how far consumers have the willingness to encourage businesses to adopt more sustainably-developed tourism, especially if it means paying higher prices.

Future Challenges

To achieve the goals and challenges set for the tourism industry as it continues to grow throughout the coming decades, will require a strong and co-operative partnership between government departments, national tourism authorities, international and national trade associations, trade unions and the tourism private sector. All stakeholders now need to share the responsibility for tourism's future and need to deliver the following to ensure its sustainability:

Governments need to:

— integrate tourism policy, especially the environment, into broader government policies;

— set up realistic capacities within sustainability frameworks, which have been set in consultation with industry and other stakeholders;

— create incentives for the tourism industry backed up where necessary by effective regulation;

— be committed to the controlled expansion, where appropriate, of infrastructure;

— apply environmental taxes fairly and nondiscriminatorily, where needed.They should be carefully thought out to minimise their impact on economic development, and revenues should be allocated to travel- and tourism-associated environment improvement programmes;

— set up mechanisms to support SMEs in the adoption of sustainable good practice;

— design policies creating incentives for corporate social responsibility in tourism, favouring a sensitive and engaging approach towards the local communities at the destinations, especially in the developing countries.

Public-private partnerships need to:

— plan and develop infrastructure with a long-term view and within a reference framework based on Agenda 21;

— implement indicators and environmental impact assessment tools to enable successful and effective local management and appropriate development;

— agree on common standards and tools to enable the measurement of progress towards achieving sustainable development;

— fund and develop contemporary research into sustainable tourism. Issues requiring attention include design, carrying capacity, tour operator activities, environmental reporting, and auditing and environmental impact assessments, socio-economic sustainability of the tourism businesses.

International bodies need to:

— co-ordinate environmental action to be undertaken by all sectors of the tourism industry, at an international level;

— review existing voluntary initiatives to improve the quality of reporting, their transparency and credibility, and the assessment of their contribution to sustainability;

— ensure that all funding, from international, national and local funding bodies, should be dependent on sound environmental practice;

— encourage and support multi-stakeholder projects aiming for sustainable tourism development;

— set up mechanisms to support the adoption of sustainable good practices by SMEs.

Private sector companies need to:

— commit to place sustainable development issues at the core of the management structure;

— develop and more widely apply certification criteria to industry initiatives;

— innovate processes and applications through new technology;
— make a commitment to the education and environmental training of staff;
— encourage corporate citizenship as the standard for private sector companies;
— be willing to engage in multi-stakeholder dialogue.

Towards Responsible Tourism

Tourism is an important factor in the management of many protected natural areas, including many biosphere reserves. Yet tourism is ambivalent, by its very nature. On the one hand, tourism generates well-known advantages. Visitor fees, concessions, and donations provide funds for restoration and protection efforts. Visitors are recruited as 'friends' of a site and can aid in generating international support. Tour operators and hotel chains can play a role in the management of a site either with financial contributions, aiding monitoring efforts, or encouraging their clients to follow guidelines of responsible tourism. Tourists can support artisan activities and help to strengthen threatened cultural values.

Tourism also generates well-known problems. Tourism growth is difficult to control. Guiding development is a time-consuming process involving establishing policies, ongoing dialogue with stakeholders, and monitoring to determine if desired conditions are being met. Tourism activities require environmental impact assessments and carrying capacity studies. At sites with limited budgets and staff, increasing tourism can stretch scarce resources taking managers away from protection efforts.

While tourism's benefits can contribute to protection and restoration efforts, it can be difficult to strike a balance between economic gain and unacceptable impacts. Managers know that a tourist attraction must be periodically renewed to remain competitive. They are also aware that actions can change an area and they are under an obligation to maintain or restore the site's original values. This poses difficult questions as to the degree of change that should be permitted to accommodate tourism growth. In addition, a further problem has been that of establishing mechanisms to enable a portion of tourism revenue to remain at the site and in the surrounding communities so as to better enable the implementation of local protection, conservation and restoration efforts.

Within UNESCO, several initiatives seek to promote a new tourism culture, based on common sense and the responsible use of the natural resources and cultural assets of each destination. Joint activities have been carried out with such bodies as the Institute of Responsible Tourism, an independent body created after the World Conference on Sustainable Tourism with the aim of encouraging sustainable development and the protection of the world's natural and cultural heritage in the field of the tourism industry. A follow-up conference on 'Sustainable Hotels for Sustainable Tourism' was held in October 2000 in Gran Canaria.

Another example is the Tour Operators' Initiative for Sustainable Tourism Development - launched in March 2000 in co-operation with UNEP, UNESCO and WTO - to create synergy between tour operators who share a common goal to develop and implement tools and practices that improve the environmental, social and cultural sustainability of tourism. The initiative highlights the benefits of sustainable tourism for tour operators and the tourism industry, and promotes practical actions for the implementation of sustainable tourism development.

The World Heritage Centre is engaged in a number of tourism related activities, including the effects of tourism development projects on the inscribed values of individual sites, such as the impact of tourism on the wildlife of the Galápagos Islands.

Several international NGOs affiliated to UNESCO have also carried out projects linked to tourism in particular regions and settings. An example is the work of the International Scientific Council for Island Development (INSULA), which in November 1999 published a study on the development and impacts of tourism and tourism services (e.g. air services) on small islands. Another example is a study on the effects on tourism on biodiversity in coastal and island regions, being carried out by ICSU's Scientific Committee on Problems of the Environment (SCOPE) and its project on 'Environment in a Global Information Society'(EGIS).

Within this broader concern for tourism interactions with the natural and cultural environment and protected natural areas, many individual and regional groups of biosphere reserves have given special attention to tourism and tourists, as reflected in the following sampling of field situations.

In East Asia, a comparative study of ecotourism has been carried out in the countries participating in the East Asian Biosphere Reserve Network, with a set of principles and guidelines elaborated for use and adaptation in participating biosphere reserves in the countries concerned. In the vast majority of the individual sites concerned, tourism is of major economic and environmental concern.

For example, with some 3 million visitors each year, Mount Sorak in the Republic of Korea has received considerable investment in infrastructure development, including access roads, consolidated facility areas, nature trails, shelter and management buildings camp sites, parking areas, drinking water and waste disposal facilities, and so on. There has also been considerable national debate and action concerning ways and means of minimizing the negative impacts of tourists and tourism on the site, such as the closure of hiking trails during the two dry seasons and the monitoring of impacts on forest regeneration.

Also in East Asia, eco-tourism is an important and increasing economic activity in many of China's biosphere reserves. At Juizhaigou Biosphere Reserve in Sichuan Province, visitor numbers have increased sharply with the building of a new road from Chengdu to Juizhaigou, from 181,000 in 1997 to 580,000 in 1999. Increased tourism has raised local annual incomes considerably, from an average per capita of 2,000 yuan in 1995, to 4,000 yuan in 1998 and 10,000 yuan in 1999, six times the average income of farmers in Sichuan Province.

The annual revenue generated through entrance tickets issued by the Juizhaigou Biosphere Reserve Administration, has also increased considerably, to 46.9 million yuan in 1999. The tax paid by Juizhaigou Biosphere Reserve to the county government rose from 2.8 million yuan in 1997 to 11.5 million yuan in 1999, representing about 80% of the total annual taxes collected by the county government in that year. Among the recent developments at Juizhaigou has been the development of an information and interpretation centre for visitors, with the costs of nearly 30 million yuan being entirely covered by the Jiuzhaigou Biosphere Reserve.

Local people have become widely involved in tourism operations, including family-run hotels and restaurants, horse and yak riding, cultural performances, handicraft shops, and so on. A new 'green bus' company has been set up through a stock-sharing mechanism. Outstanding problems and challenges at Juizhaigou include overcrowding of the more popular tourist areas, still-inadequate tour-guide training and educational facilities, and the operation of some non-environment-friendly businesses in the biosphere reserve area.

The identification of best practices in the hotel and catering industry has received attention in a number of reserves. An example is on the Baltic island of Hiiumaa (part of the West Estonian Archipelago Biosphere Reserve), where a process of environmentally friendly tourism has been initiated by the island councils for tourism and for environmental protection, the biosphere reserve administration, the Hiiumaa Tourism Association and tourism companies. Those involved in local tourism found that co-operation with nature protection interests was a vital factor in establishing a niche for tourism on the island, and in being able to compete with large mainland and international firms.

This collaborative understanding led to the idea of establishing a Green Label scheme for identifying environment-friendly products and services. Six criteria were used for awarding the Green Label for accommodation and restuarant services, covering such issues as waste management, reduction of plastic packaging through increased use of local products, measures for economizing the use of water and electricity, identification and use of more environment-friendly chemicals and consumption of locally produced food. The initial results of the introduction of the Green Label have been encouraging: one poll of tourists showed that 50% of visitors to Hiiumaa were aware of the Green Label scheme and that out of these tourists 70% had chosen accommodation with the Green Label commendation.

The degradation of trail resources associated with expanding recreation and tourism visitation is a growing management problem in many biosphere reserves worldwide. In order to make judicious trail and visitor management decisions, reserve managers need objective and timely information on trail resource conditions. Within such a perspective, a 'trail problem-assessment survey' method has been tested within the Great Smoky Mountains National Park, part of the Southern Appalachian Biosphere Reserve along the Tennessee and North Carolina state border in the United States. The method characterizes the location and lineal extent of common trail problems. It employs a continuous search for multiple indicators of pre-defined tread problems, yielding census data documenting the location, occurrence and extent of each problem.

Twenty-three different indicators in three categories were used to gather inventory, resource condition, and design and maintenance data for each of 72 hiking trails totalling 528 km (35% of the park's total trail length). Soil erosion and wet soil were found to be most common impacts on a linear extent basis. Other findings related to such aspects as the distribution of trails with serious tread problems and the effectiveness of maintenance features installed to divert water from trail treads. More generally, the trail problem-assessment method might be considered by managers of biosphere reserves in regions with different environmental and impact characteristics.

In recent years the UN has begun to make travel and tourism a priority in the sustainable development debate. In 1999,WTTC and IH&RA were designated by the United Nations Commission on Sustainable Development to represent the industry in a multi-stakeholder dialogue at its seventh session. It was concluded that voluntary measures developed with multistakeholder participation, mutual trust and respect, transparency, monitoring, and assessment and verification were seen as most likely to generate confidence and support from all parties'.

The travel and tourism industry increasingly recognises the need for protecting culture, heritage and the environment and this responsibility must be shared by all stakeholders. It also needs to be balanced by a proportionate recognition that travel and tourism has the potential to bring social and environmental, as well as economic benefits. This would give developing countries the possibility to attain the full economic potential tourism can give.This must be coupled with sufficient training in management skills and education for local people.The human resources issue will be of much concern in the next few years because, without substantial and skilled human capital, the tourism industry cannot be productive in the future.

Adequate planning and development is also vital so that fragile eco-systems and scarce natural resources can be utilised effectively and protected for future generations. Moreover, the prevailing issues facing infrastructure are becoming more acute with the continuing increase in passenger travel.

Governmental infrastructure constraints pose a critical barrier and can jeopardise anticipated economic growth and job creation with knock-on effects to all sectors of the community. The fundamental infrastructure issues such as airport congestion, air traffic management, sources of capital investment, regulation and political support, and institutional reform facing the sustainable development and growth of travel and tourism, concern both the private and public sectors.

Governments are beginning to take a more dynamic role in developing sustainable and economically-successful tourism, but there urgently needs to be more proactive participation from government.With effective networking processes, legitimate policies, planning and development from government, tourism can alter its adverse environmental image to one of sustainability and stewardship. The many and varied voluntary industry initiatives, ranging from education to certification, are an important and imperative part of the ongoing process working towards sustainable development.

2

Ecological Approach to Tourism Management

Tourism is continuing to grow rapidly, despite some regional and year-to-year fluctuations, and an enormous increase is forecast for international tourism over the next 25 years. In 2000, there were an estimated 698 million international tourists: 1.6 billion international tourists are forecast by 2020. Expansion of tourism affects all regions, including in remote and sensitive areas such as islands, coasts and new mountain areas, and Antarctica, as well as species-rich and protected areas, and urban areas. Furthermore, tourism based on the natural environment is a vital and growing segment of the tourism industry. The statistics of tourism growth underline the large and growing pressures that tourism is placing on the environment and biodiversity.

For many countries, tourism is an important source of foreign exchange and a major contributor to gross national product (GNP), that may offer a real alternative to other more obviously detrimental forms of development. At local and national levels, tourism can lead to investment in infrastructure with benefits that spread beyond tourism, and can provide a rationale for promoting environmental protection. While beaches and mountains, rivers, forests and biodiversity make the environment a basic resource upon which the tourism industry depends to thrive and grow, tourism also has important adverse environmental impacts as a result of resource consumption, as well as from pollution and wastes generated by tourism activities, including transport.

Types of Tourism

Tourism can be described as the activities of persons travelling to and/or staying in places outside of their usual environment for leisure, business or other purposes (including visits to friends and relatives).

Tourism may be planned and/or organized in two main ways:

(a) Individual travel is a journey organized by a traveller, either directly or with help of a provider of tourism services, a tour operator or a travel agency;

(b) A package tour is a pre-arranged combination of not fewer than two of the following tourism services when sold or offered for sale at an inclusive price and when the service covers a period of more than 24 hours or includes overnight accommodation: - transport, accommodation, other tourism services not ancillary to transport or accommodation and accounting for a significant proportion of the package tour.

Furthermore, while international tourism - where tourists travel from their home country to a different host country - often receives most attention, domestic tourism within a country is generally far larger in terms of numbers of tourists, and generates considerable impacts. It is important to note that the World Tourism Organization emphasizes that all tourism activities, whether related to holidays, business, conferences, congresses or fairs, health, adventure or ecotourism, must be sustainable.

All forms of tourism have a certain negative impact on biodiversity if not planned and managed well. Although there are no formal definitions of different forms of tourism, the following descriptions represent a brief selection of the various forms of tourism (many of which overlap with one another) that can be identified within the overall tourism sector:

Nature-based tourism involves individual and/or organized tours into natural areas. The World Tourism Organization describes ecotourism in the following terms: "Ecotourism is tourism practised in relatively undisturbed natural areas, for the main purpose of admiring and learning about them". In the past, there has been confusion over the relationship of ecotourism to sustainable tourism, and some have regarded ecotourism as sustainable tourism with a focus on nature. It is therefore important to understand that ecotourism is just one of many forms of tourism, and that all forms of tourism, including ecotourism, must become sustainable. An activity that is described as "ecotourism" is not per se sustainable. The activities involved in nature-based tourism are diverse and include hiking/trekking tours, hunting tours (on foot), safari tours (by car or on foot), marine-watching tours (by boat, and including scuba-diving).

Active holidays or sports tourism are focused on sports activities during the holiday, for example in winter: skiing, cross-country-skiing, snow hiking, snowboarding etc., and in summer: on the ground: cycling, hiking, horse-riding, mountaineering, etc., in the air: paragliding, etc., and on/in the water: rafting, canyoning, scuba diving, skin-diving, sailing, surfing, etc. Sports activities and tourism are intrinsically linked to sound environmental conditions and to the long-term maintenance of landscape qualities, and the principle of sustainability applies as much to sports tourism as to other forms of tourism. It is important that sportsmen and sportswomen as well as sports tourists in their own interests identify themselves with the aims of nature conservation and environmental protection and commit themselves to observing appropriate restrictions, assuming themselves responsibility for it.

Landscape and environmental resources must be utilized with awareness. This is the only way to prevent the principle of sustainability from being negligently infringed in specific situations. If a sportsman/ sportswoman or sports tourist does not or cannot recognize such a situation of conflicting uses, responsibilities, criteria and measures must be developed and recognised in order to prevent them.

Beach- and coastal-based tourism, which is focused on "sun, sea and sand" and involves very dense development concentrated in coastal resorts. The main activities are relaxation with some watersports. The concentration of development which reflects the huge demand for this form of tourism has had major impacts in many parts of the world, including the Caribbean, the Mediterranean basin (which receives around 30 per cent of all international tourist arrivals), and South-East Asia, as well as in resort areas elsewhere. Impacts include the effects of hotels and infrastructure development, damage to coastal ecosystems, and impacts from waste generation and from the massive scale of visitation.

Mountain-based tourism, including alpine/high mountain tourism involving skiing and winter sports during winter months, and walking during the summer months, particularly in Europe, trekking in mountain regions, such as the Himalayas, is also extremely popular, and has led to the development of mountain resorts and trekking routes in many mountainous regions of the world. The scale of development in the context of mountain ecosystems that are often fragile, can result in serious impacts on the environment and biodiversity in areas where mountain tourism takes place.

Cultural tourism focuses mainly on the cultural and traditional heritage of populations. It is mainly based around ancient relics and historical sites, as well as attractions that demonstrate old traditions in action. It further encompasses contemporary cultural events, museums and similar facilities. This form of tourism is most visible in towns and cities where these cultural attractions are concentrated, as well as around major historical sites. Frequent visits to attractions in remote areas can result in enormous negative impacts on the cultural and biological diversity.

Ethno-tourism: Traditional/indigenous comnıunities and their folklore, buildings, economic life, handicrafts, shrines.

Rural tourism (agro-tourism): Interest lies in special cultural manifestationsin a rural context, or at least in one close to nature, including rural estates (e.g. fincas), interesting villages, cultural landscapes and farming activities (e.g. rice terraces); horse-back-riding

Educational tourism: Courses and workshops (music, handicrafts, languages, natural medicine, etc.), based upon authentic local capabilities

Nature tourism: Interest lies in diverse nature, pristine at best

Scientific tourism: Interest lies in visiting social or ecological projectsand trips for professional or educational purposes

Religious/esoteric tourism: Traditional places of pilgrimage, monasteries and other sacred places, traditional ceremonies, meditation centres, etc.

Health tourism/ weekend-outings: Thermal or mineral baths, cool mountain areas in tropical countries

Chain of Tourism

Tourism and travel form multi-component products that consist of a number of individual goods and services which are utilized in various phases of a process, also called the tourism chain. Distinguishing the five phases of the tourism chain helps in the analysis of the impact of tourism:

(a) Preparation of a trip:

— Wish to travel: media, advertising, information;

— Search for offers, booking: travel office, travel agent, telecommunications;

— Baggage, equipment, hobby articles: industry and commerce;

(b) Travel to destination:

— Transportation: car, bus, rail, airplane;

(c) Stay at destination:

(i) Accommodation: hotel and other facilities;

(ii) Meals: restaurants, self-catering;

(iii) Leisure-time activities and consumption at site:

— Industry/commerce, transportation, other services;

— Cultural activities;

— Activities on land: hiking, cycling, horseback riding, etc.

— Activities in and on the water: swimming, diving, canoe/ kayak, surfing, sailing;

— Activities in the air: gliders, parachutes, hang-gliders, etc.

— Activities at special facilities: golf, indoor swimming, squash, theme parks, etc.

(d) Return travel home:

— Transportation: car, bus, rail, airplane

(e) Post-travel activities:

— Washing/drycleaning/ repair of equipment etc., developing photos, etc.: industry/ commerce

Many of the goods and services are only partially or indirectly connected with tourism, so that the product specifics of tourism must be given particular attention and a trip should be considered in its complexity.

Stakeholders Involved in Tourism

A wide range of stakeholders are involved in tourism, including:

(a) Governments at central and regional level;

(b) Local authorities at destinations;

(c) Local communities in and around destinations including indigenous communities;

(d) The tourism sector - private sector directly:

(i) Tour operators;

(ii) Tourism developers;

(iii) Hotel operators;

(iv) Facilities operators;

(v) Transport operators;

(e) Sectors providing goods and services for tourism (e.g., food)

(f) Sectors that may be affected adversely by tourism (e.g., artisanal fisheries);

(g) Tourists.

The wide range of stakeholders involved in tourism - governments at central and local level, local authorities, the tourism sector, as well as other sectors providing goods and services for tourism, and tourists themselves - have a shared responsibility to make tourism sustainable. To achieve change towards more sustainable tourism, programmes on both the supply and demand sides need to be established: for example, capacity development work with local authorities, dissemination of best practice and support for technical cooperation to both public authorities and the private sector, and awareness raising programmes aimed at changing the behaviour of tourists. Despite some progress by various stakeholders there is an urgent need to improve the way tourism is developed and managed.

Relationship of Tourism with Biodiversity

The global social, economic and environmental impacts of tourism are immense and highly complex. International tourism operates in an increasingly global market in which investors and tourists have an ever-widening choice of destinations, and the international tourism market is fiercely competitive, much of it operating on low profit margins. For this reason, self-regulation of the tourism industry for sustainable use of biological resources has only rarely been successful.

Tourism contributes to economic development through funding the development of infrastructure and services, providing jobs, providing funds for development or maintenance of sustainable practices, providing alternative and supplementary ways for communities to receive revenue from biological diversity, and generating incomes.

At the same time, tourism results in environmental impacts on land and resources, including impacts on vegetation, wildlife, and ecosystems, and impacts arising from waste management and travel and transport; and in socio-economic and cultural impacts that affect local communities, social relations and cultural values. Such socio-economic and cultural impacts may damage lifestyles and practices that contribute to the conservation and sustainable use of biodiversity.

However, the assessment also recognizes the significant potential of tourism for realizing benefits in terms of the conservation of biological diversity and the sustainable use of its components, and for contributing to public education and awareness of these issues.

The assessment follows up on findings expressed, for example in the 1997 Berlin Declaration on Biological Diversity and Tourism, which notes that:

(a) Tourism has a large and growing importance for economic development, and can generate income for local communities, including indigenous communities;

(b) Tourism is largely based on a healthy environment and beautiful landscapes;

(c) Tourism increasingly turns to relatively undisturbed natural areas;

(d) Tourism has the potential for degrading the natural environment, social structures and cultural heritage;

(e) Tourism may generate or increase a demand for wild animals, plants or products for souvenirs which may endanger species and affect protection measures;

(f) Tourism can serve as a major educational opportunity, increasing knowledge of natural ecosystems and local communities;

(g) Tourism can create revenues for the maintenance of natural areas;

(h) Self-regulation of the tourism industry for sustainable use of biological resources has rarely been successful because of its economics and financial interests far away from destinations.

The Convention on Biological Diversity describes biological diversity as "the variability among living organisms from all sources including, inter alia, terrestrial, marine and other aquatic ecosystems and the ecological complexes of which they are part; this includes diversity within species, between species and of ecosystems". In other words, biodiversity is the variability of life in all forms, levels and combinations. It is not the sum of all ecosystems, species and genetic material. Rather, it represents the variability among and within them. It is, therefore, an attribute of life, contrasting with "biological resources", which are tangible biotic components of ecosystems.

Biological resources are described in the Convention on Biological Diversity as including "genetic resources, organisms or parts thereof, populations or any other biotic component of ecosystems with actual or potential use value for humanity." In addition, the preamble to the Convention refers to the "... intrinsic value of biological diversity and of the ecological, genetic, social, economic, scientific, educational, cultural, recreational and aesthetic values of biological diversity and its components". The intrinsic educational, cultural, recreational and aesthetic values of biological diversity and its components are particularly important aspects for tourism.

Landscape diversity - the variety of landscapes within a region and the diversity of elements and processes within and among these landscapes, which are homogenous ecological units defined by distinctive combinations of elements that include landform, climate, geology and vegetation / - is also important for tourism.

The Convention on Biological Diversity contains a series of far-reaching provisions on the conservation of biological diversity, on the sustainable use of the components of biological diversity, and on access and benefit sharing, as well as important provisions that recognise the role of indigenous and local communities in the conservation and sustainable use of biological diversity. For indigenous and local communities there often is a strong and unified connection between their socio-economic activities, cultural values and biological diversity, which is a significant element in their livelihoods. Frequently, the knowledge and resources of indigenous, traditional and local communities has been appropriate without the sharing of benefits, without their prior informed consent, without full disclosure of proposed activities and without respect for the rights of these communities and individuals.

Local Communities and Biodiversity

There are strong connections between indigenous and local communities and biodiversity. The cultural and management practices of these communities can be extremely important for the conservation and sustainable use of biodiversity, and this is often central to their livelihoods.

Indigenous and local communities are to be considered significant stakeholders in any tourism operations or proposed tourism developments taking place within their traditional territories and are therefore to be accorded the same respect as any other stakeholders in all stages of the development, operation and management of such tourism activities/enterprises.

Article 8(j) of the Convention on Biological Diversity addresses the need to "respect, preserve and maintain knowledge, innovations and practices of indigenous and local communities embodying traditional lifestyles relevant for the conservation and sustainable use of biological diversity" and to "encourage the equitable sharing of benefits arising from the utilization of such knowledge, innovations and practices" of these groups.

With a view to implementing Article 8(j) of the Convention, the Conference of the Parties, through various bodies established under the Convention, is in the process of developing guidelines with regard to:

(a) The recognition, safeguarding and fully guaranteeing of the rights of indigenous and local communities over their traditional knowledge, innovations and practices within the context of the Convention;

(b) Effective participation of indigenous and local communities in decision-making, policy planning and development and implementation of the conservation and sustainable use of biological diversity;

(c) Access and benefit sharing;

(d) Prior informed consent;

(e) Ethical conduct with regard to research, access to, use, exchange and management of information concerning traditional knowledge, innovations and practices;

(f) National incentive schemes for indigenous and local communities to preserve and maintain their traditional knowledge, innovations and practices and for their application in national strategies and programmes for the conservation and sustainable use of biological diversity;

(g) The conduct of cultural, environmental and social impact assessments regarding any development proposed to take place on sacred sites and on lands or waters occupied or used by indigenous and local communities; and

(h) Use of traditional knowledge for the conservation and sustainable use of biological diversity in a range of contexts (for example, ecosystem approach, in situ conservation, biodiversity monitoring and environmental impact assessments).

The development of any tourism guidelines should take into account the relevant guidelines being developed under the Convention on Biological Diversity and seek to harmonize such guidelines with them. In this context, it is important to emphasise the need for participation of local and indigenous communities, not only in policy development but also in the benefits derived from tourism.

Gender Issues

Gender issues are also important in relation to guidelines on tourism and biodiversity. Women have an important role in tourism, representing on average half of all employees in tourism enterprises, although there are wide variations in this figure among enterprises, and being employed frequently in poorly paid and insecure jobs in the tourism sector. In many areas, women also play a significant part in the management of biodiversity resources.

Ecosystem Approach to Tourism

The ecosystem approach is a strategy for the integrated management of land, water and living resources that promotes conservation and sustainable use in an equitable way. Thus, the application of the ecosystem approach will help to reach a balance of the three objectives of the Convention: conservation; sustainable use; and the fair and equitable sharing of the benefits arising out of the utilization of genetic resources. The approach is based on the application of appropriate scientific methodologies focused on levels of biological organization, which encompass the essential structure, processes, functions and interactions among organisms and their environment. It recognizes that humans, with their cultural diversity, are an integral component of many ecosystems.

Principles and Operational Guidance

The ecosystem approach comprises twelve principles and five operational guidance elements. The following are the principles and operational guidance elements of ecosystem approach:

Principles

Principle 1: The objectives of management of land, water and living resources are a matter of societal choice.

Principle 2: Management should be decentralized to the lowest appropriate level.

A broad consensus relative to the planning and management of sustainable tourism by all stakeholders, affected and interested groups, is the basis for future and long-term success. Therefore the objectives of management are a matter of societal choices and have to be decentralized to the lowest appropriate level, by involvement and participation of all stakeholders.

Principle 3: Ecosystem managers should consider the effects

A flexible mix of instruments should be established for the continuous monitoring of actual impacts and research of potential impacts on ecosystems caused by tourism development. No development should take place without adequate baseline research and information, and environmental impact assessments, including assessment of cumulative impacts and alternative options, leading to conditions being set for management to avoid or minimise anticipated impacts. Integrated land use management should be modified to take into account information and research on actual and potential impacts.

Principle 4: Recognizing potential gains from management, there is usually a need to understand and manage the ecosystem in an economic context. Any such ecosystem-management programme should:

a) Reduce those market distortions that adversely affect biological diversity;

Market distortions that have led to tourism activities that have damaged the environment and biodiversity, should be removed, and measures introduced to restore damaged areas and to apply integrated management approaches to all land management including tourism activities. This goes also for goods and services of ecosystems related to the tourism market.

b) Align incentives to promote biodiversity conservation and sustainable use;

To support the conservation of ecosystems and discourage negative impacts all possible incentives for the development and running of sustainable tourism should be established by governments and local authorities, and should be consistent with national and local objectives for biodiversity.

c) Internalize costs and benefits in the given ecosystem to the extent feasible.

All environmental costs and benefits of tourism activities should be taken into account. The internalization of external costs is an important element for the successful management of sustainable tourism.

Principle 5: Conservation of ecosystem structure and functioning, in order to maintain ecosystem services, should be a priority target of the ecosystem approach.

Intact ecosystems and biodiversity are important in providing the quality environments on which tourism depends, and tourism should contribute to their conservation, restore any past damage associated with tourism, and minimise adverse effects.

Principle 6: Ecosystem must be managed within the limits of their functioning.

All tourism development should be established only on the basis of accurate research and information concerning all affected areas and ecosystems, and including baseline information on areas and their functioning, indigenous and traditional knowledge, impact assessment of proposals for tourism development, and impact management measures to minimise adverse impacts. Based on this research and information, appropriate restrictions and conditions should be placed on tourism and other developments to protect biodiversity and to ensure a balance between sustainable tourism and biodiversity.

Principle 7: The ecosystem approach should be undertaken at the appropriate spatial and temporal scales.

As described in relation to Principles 1 and 2 of the Ecosystem Approach, the boundaries for management of ecosystems and the sustainable use (Links to analysis of sustainable tourism principles, etc: tourism) need to be defined operationally by users, managers, scientists and indigenous and local communities.

Principle 8: Recognizing the varying temporal scales and lag-effects that characterize ecosystem processes, objectives for ecosystem management should be set for the long term.

This is a very important factor in relation to tourism and biodiversity, and the support of management of ecosystems and their sustainable use by providing policies and frameworks on different levels should not be hindered by short-term processes. Because of these factors and the complexity of the systems involved, the responses are also complex and non-linear (Links to analysis of sustainable tourism principles, etc: in other words, a small change in one place can lead to a much larger change somewhere else, through a complex chain of events). This means that management must work through networks of linkages, and look for the most effective points for management interventions, which may not always be the points nearest to the observed problems to be addressed.

Principle 9: Management must recognize that change is inevitable.

Both tourism and biodiversity are highly dynamic, and therefore regular monitoring and use indicators are important in management to ensure that tourism and biodiversity remain in balance, and that overall goals and objectives are reached.

Principle 10: The ecosystem approach should seek the appropriate balance between, and integration of, conservation and use of biological diversity.

A balanced co-existence needs to be achieved between the use and the conservation of ecosystems, and tourism activities, in all areas. This requires an integrated approach to land use management, that incorporates biodiversity conservation and sustainable use, and sustainable tourism. This approach to land use management needs to take into account the requirements for ecosystem functioning and of habitat integrity and interconnections that are required for conservation of viable populations of species.

Principle 11: The ecosystem approach should consider all forms of relevant information, including scientific and indigenous and local knowledge, innovations and practices.

Principle 12: The ecosystem approach should involve all relevant sectors of society and scientific disciplines.

All stakeholders should co-operate and exchange all forms of relevant information at all levels for a better understanding, planning and management of sustainable tourism in ecosystems. In all cases of operation, management and development of tourism activities, the traditional biodiversity-related knowledge, innovations and practices of indigenous and local communities must be respected, as set out in Article 8j of the Convention on Biological Diversity.

Operational guidance

Guidance 1: Focus on the relationships and processes within ecosystem.

All efforts should be made for more effective and coordinated research, monitoring and assessment about the impacts of tourism activities in ecosystems. The distribution of the results should lead to better management practices, planning processes and the development of strategies and policies.

Guidance 2: Enhance benefit-sharing.

The equitable sharing of benefits with host communities where tourism takes place, especially indigenous and local communities, who are affected by and/or involved in tourism activities, is an important part of the management and sustainable use of ecosystems, and of making tourism sustainable.

Guidance 3: Use adaptive management practices.

Ecosystem management needs to recognize the diversity of social and cultural factors, as well as environmental and ecological factors, and their interaction with socio-economic and cultural factors affecting natural-resource use. Prior information exchange, training and capacity building of people involved about sustainable tourism practices in ecosystem management has to be established. Management of tourism development and activities should also take into account ongoing monitoring of effects on the environment and biodiversity, and make adjustments that incorporate lessons learned, so as to achieve the objectives of sustainable tourism and biodiversity conservation and sustainable use.

Guidance 4: Carry out management actions at the scale appropriate for the issue being addressed, with decentralization to lowest level, as appropriate.

Empower local people, to be involved in the planning and management of sustainable tourism activities, through capacity building, and by creating a strong framework for decision-making incorporating public participation of the broader community, within which responsibilities and management can be undertaken by, or as close to, affected communities and areas as appropriate for good administration.

Guidance 5: Ensure intersectoral cooperation.

The ecosystem approach and the sustainable use of resources has to be recognized as a cross-cutting issue and should be integrated into related strategies and activities. Therefore information exchange and intersectoral cooperation at all levels should be established regarding the implementation of sustainable tourism practices and policies.

Agreements on Sustainable Tourism and Biodiversity

Sustainable tourism can be considered as tourism that puts sustainable development into practice in its development and operations. It is therefore important to consider the approach to sustainable development as a first step in understanding how such an approach can be applied in relation to tourism, leading to tourism that is itself sustainable.

In 1996, the International Council for Local Environmental Initiatives (ICLEI), which represents local government at international level, adopted a description of sustainable development that contains some more specific elements relating to how the vision of sustainable development may be achieved in practice, especially in relation to the communities served by local government. The ICLEI approach specifies that at a minimum, sustainable development should deliver basic services to residents in any community, and should not threaten delivery of these services.

The concept of sustainable livelihoods is also relevant to understanding a definition of sustainable development at a local level. This concept has been adopted by the United Nations Development Programme and in bilateral aid programmes, such as that of the

United Kingdom Department for International Development.

The sustainable livelihood concept focuses attention on those elements that families and communities require as a means for living and specifies that the natural resource base should not be undermined. It addresses the levels of those elements that are necessary to prevent their means for living from being vulnerable to the combined consequences of stresses and shocks. These include the stresses that they may place on their local environment and those of external events outside of their control.

Taken together, the description of sustainable development provided by ICLEI, and the concept of sustainable livelihoods are both important in the context of tourism. Most of the impacts of tourism are felt at the local level in and around areas visited by tourists. If tourism is to contribute to sustainable development at a local level, these descriptions of sustainable development would require that it should lead to adequate delivery of basic environmental, social and economic services to all residents of a community. It should provide sustainable livelihoods without undermining the viability of the natural, built and social systems and resources.

In applying these concepts of sustainable tourism it is important to recall that such concepts and principles cannot be applied directly or uniformly in any given setting: they require reinterpretation to take into account the particular context to which they are being applied. / Furthermore, each setting is subject to change and fluctuations which impose stresses and shocks. To be sustainable, development must remain sustainable in the face of such stresses and shocks, which highlights the need for long-term plans that incorporate sufficient margins to cope with inevitable stresses and shocks that any area and its constituent communities will face over time. It should also be noted that eco-tourism, which incorporates an emphasis on sustainability, represents a type of tourism that is based on the natural environment, and that all types of tourism, including eco-tourism, should be sustainable.

A number of conventions now in force address various aspects of biological diversity conservation. Together with the Convention on Biological Diversity, they form the regime applicable to biological diversity. They include major global instruments of particular relevance in relation to tourism and biodiversity.

Convention Concerning the Protection of the World Cultural and Natural Heritage

The World Heritage Convention requires parties to take steps to identify, protect, conserve, present and transmit to future generations the cultural and natural heritage within their territories. Cultural and natural areas of outstanding universal value are eligible for listing on the World Heritage List and the Convention establishes the World Heritage Fund which can be used by the World Heritage Committee to assist countries with establishing and conserving World Heritage Sites.

World Heritage Sites can be a major attraction for tourism, and revenue from tourism can contribute to their maintenance and preservation. However, such sites are vulnerable to pressures from tourism, and a survey of management problems at World Heritage Sites fully or partly designated for their natural heritage, found that between 16-63 percent (varying according to continent) experienced problems arising from tourism, and that inadequate or insufficient management, mainly resulting from low funding, was also a common problem. Problems arising from an imbalance between management capacity and tourism pressures are serious, since strong management planning and control is an essential factor in ensuring that visitation remains within the bounds of resource limits

Convention on International Trade in Endangered Species of Wild Fauna and Flora (CITES)

CITES regulates international trade of all species listed in its appendices. Appendix I lists species threatened with extinction which are or may be affected by trade. Trade in these species is banned except in exceptional circumstances, in accordance with the provisions of the Convention. Appendix II lists species not yet threatened with extinction, but which may become so unless their trade is subject to strict international controls. Appendix III lists species which any party identifies as subject to regulation within its jurisdiction to prevent or restrict exploitation, and which require the cooperation of the other CITES parties in the control of international trade.

In the past, some tourist souvenirs and handicrafts have incorporated endangered species. Strong vigilance by national and customs authorities in enforcing CITES, coupled with awareness-raising campaigns targeted at international tourists, has had a major effect on reducing the trade in endangered species in the context of tourism.

Convention on Wetlands of International Importance Especially as Waterfowl Habitat

The Ramsar Convention requires each party to promote the conservation of internationally important wetlands and the wise use of all wetlands within its territory. Conservation measures are to be established in wetland areas to promote wetland and waterfowl conservation. Each party designates at least one wetland area of international significance to be included on the world list maintained under the Convention.

Wetlands can be important as habitats that attract tourists, and may also be threatened by tourism development through reclamation of land for construction of tourism facilities and infrastructure, and through extraction of water to support tourism activities.

International Guidelines to Sustainable Tourism

A wide range of codes, guidelines, principles and position papers are existing at the international level and also some at the regional level, that relate to sustainable tourism, and including some that refer specifically to sustainable tourism and biodiversity. Some of them are:

— Code of Ethics for Tourists, CCA, Penang, 1975

— Manila Declaration, CCA, Manila, 1980

— Manila Declaration on World Tourism, World Tourism Organization (WTO/OMT), Manila, 1980

— Charter for Sustainable Tourism, Lanzarote, 1995

— The European Charter for Sustainable Tourism , Federation of Nature and Natural Parks of Europe, 1997

— World Congress Against the Commercial Sexual Exploitation of Children - Agenda for Action, Stockholm, 1996

— Manila Declaration on the Social Impact of Tourism, WTO/OMT, Manila, 1997.

— Malé Declaration on Sustainable Tourism Development, Asia-Pacific Ministers Conference, WTO/OMT, Malé 1997.

— Berlin Declaration, Berlin 1997.

— Position Paper on the Global Code of Ethics, TEN, ECTWT, Equitable Tourism Options (Equations) Stuttgart 1998

- — International Conference on sustainable tourism in Small Islands Developing States (SIDS) and other islands, Lanzarote, Spain, October 1998.
- — Agenda 21 for the Travel & Tourism Industry, World Travel and Tourism Council (WTTC), WTO/OMT, Earth Council 1998
- — Global Code of Ethics for Tourism, WTO, 1999
- — Position Paper on tourism, poverty and sustainable development to CSD-7
- — Principles for the implementation of sustainable tourism, UNEP, 2000
- — Position paper on tourism, WWF-International, 2000
- — Draft Guidelines for the Conduct of Tourism in Territories Traditionally Occupied or Used by Indigenous and Local Communities, Internal CBD document

These principles and guidelines on sustainable tourism acknowledge the importance of biodiversity, but guidance so far available is very general, and detailed technical guidance is needed on how to implement and manage tourism in relation to biodiversity. Guidelines that are formulated specifically on tourism and biodiversity focus mainly on protected areas and the requirements of protected area managers; All the principles and guidelines analysed contain extensive common and complementary elements - no cases were found where one principle or guideline was in conflict with another.

Audiences for international guidelines

The major actor groups that can influence tourism and its impacts in relation to biodiversity including governments, industry (primary tourism sector, including tourism companies, transport companies, hoteliers, provision of services and attractions; and secondary sectors linked to the tourism sector through provision of goods and services (e.g., food supply)), international organizations, non-governmental organizations, individual tourists, biodiversity and/or protected-area managers, indigenous and local communities.

Governments, international agencies (including aid agencies), and international development banks: Tourism is an increasingly important component of global, national and local economic planning and development. In developing and developed countries tourism is often the most immediately promising means to develop cash flows and local economic capacities in remote areas without substantial upfront capital investment levels which are required for industrial development.

The international guidelines on sustainable tourism should address the issues of tourism development with links to and impacts upon biological diversity and ecosystem processes - even though that tourism is not focused on appreciation of the natural environment. They address tourism "creep" whereby small-scale local nature-based tourism tends to grow towards industrial scale synthetic tourism with associated urban infrastructure demands.

The guidelines provide assistance to Governments, and other agencies, responding to pressures for tourism development and investment, in assessing proposals and in ensuring that tourism development only proceeds where it meets the objectives of sustainable development and of biodiversity conservation and sustainable use. They also provide guidance to international development agencies and funding institutions concerning priority areas for support, including capacity-building and finance, in relation to sustainable tourism and biodiversity.

Indigenous and local communities: The guidelines address the issues of managing the impacts of tourism development on the culture and resources and the biological diversity and ecological processes of the environments of indigenous and local communities. They are consistent with efforts, within the framework of the Convention on Biological Diversity, to respect, preserve and maintain traditional knowledge, and promote its wider application.

Tourism sector: The tourism industry is one of the important partners for the implementation of guidelines into the practice. The fulfilment of their given commitments would be the first step towards an open partnership between all stakeholders. The guidelines on sustainable tourism address management requirements and responsibilities of private enterprises involved in all aspects of tourism, and as a result, assist the tourism industry to put commitments to sustainable development into practice. They also set these in the wider context of the shared responsibilities of all stakeholder groups for sustainable tourism and biodiversity conservation and sustainable use.

Individual tourists: Tourists, and particularly those engaging in environmental or nature-based tourism, tend to have high levels of education and abilities to find information through the Internet. The guidelines address the rights and responsibilities of tourists in terms of quality sustainable tourism experience, of expectation that operators will maintain standards which provide sustainability and of involvement in monitoring or other supportive activities.

Non-governmental organizations: The guidelines address issues that are central to the interests of environmental non-governmental organizations. They address tourism/environment issues outside, as well as within, protected areas. They also address matters relevant to non-governmental organizations involved in regional development, poverty relief and consumer awareness.

Protected-area managers: The guidelines provide an overarching framework within which more specific and detailed guidelines for management of tourism in particular regions and sites can be incorporated easily. They cross link broader issues of environmental sustainability, impact prediction and management to matters addressed in guidelines relating to management of tourism in protected areas.

Management Approaches

Practices for Decision-making

Where tourism as an activity that threatens/impacts or has the potential to threaten/impact biodiversity, either directly, or indirectly, through other social, cultural, political or economic drivers, measures are needed to:

(a) Initiate or maintain protection of natural ecosystems;

(b) Prevent or mitigate impact to those ecosystems;

(c) Restore their integrity.

Strong frameworks for decision-making incorporating public participation involving the broader community in input to and review of decisions, including their prior informed consent, are essential for such measures if they are to work effectively. These need to operate at national, regional and site levels, and aspects to be considered in such frameworks for decision-making and public participation include:

(a) Strategic regional level appraisal of biodiversity resources, assignment of importance ratings and analysis of threat and vulnerability of biodiversity and ecological processes. A conservation plan might be the outcome;

(b) Identification of opportunities and constraints for tourism development that is linked to biodiversity resources. This considers market demand for access to particular types of resources for particular types of tourism activities. These could range from recreational mass-market demand to highly specialised niche market demand. It also must determine which types of activities each type of use without degradation of the primary resource can sustain. This could incorporate a public scoping exercise to frame the basis of and criteria for subsequent decisions. A strategic biodiversity/tourism assessment could be the outcome;

(c) Subregional planning: Usually conducted in conjunction with other land-use planning exercises, to ensure rationale allocation of biophysical resources and infrastructure, but with a specific focus on tourism and the potential impacts on biodiversity. Bioregional plans would be an outcome;

(d) Regional environmental management planning. An environmental impact management strategic analysis, identifying generic locations, levels and circumstances of acceptable impacts for permissible activities;

(e) Protected area planning: A protected area scale analysis, with a high level of detail would be desirable. Protected area conceptual development plans would be an outcome;

(f) Site-level planning: Conceptual analysis of a particular site, indicated as suitable for tourism development of a particular type, within the framework of a bioregional plan or a protected area conceptual development plan. Output is a concept proposal for a particular type of facility/activities. Nature, scale and market, activities would all be considered, as would management and mitigation measures necessary to avoid negative impacts, and ensure positive impacts;

(g) Site/activity environmental impact assessment: Detailed analysis of the potential impacts of a proposed tourism development, where the composition of the development is known, its precise location is known, and there is a detailed site plan, including all services, and nature and extent of all associated activities;

(h) Site/activity environmental management plan: Design of a detailed program of actions, timing and responsibilities for implementing measures to ensure that construction, operation and (possibly decommissioning) of a particular tourism facility/activity is conducted in accordance with the findings and recommendations of the environmental impact assessment, conceptual development plan and bioregional plan. It includes mitigation measures to prevent or limit impacts, and rehabilitation guidelines for impacted areas. It will also address a cycle of environmental audits during the construction, commissioning, operational and decommissioning stages;

(i) Strategic, regional and site level socio-economic assessments in relation to items (a) - (h) above;

(j) Assessment of the quality of information available and provided, and of the requirements for impact management, and any education, training and resourcing needs local planners, authorities, indigenous and local communities, etc., to address any gaps identified between the requirements of impact management / plan implementation, and available capacity and resources.

It is important to stress that these aspects of the decision-making and public participation framework need to be well-integrated with each other, and with broader national and regional policies, in order to function effectively. While some specific features of sustainable tourism and biodiversity can be treated individually, many are cross-cutting in terms of the issues raised, the departments and organisations involved, and the need for coordination between the various levels of decision-making.

Outline Management Steps

The following sequence of ten management steps, each of which can incorporate public participation, is suggested as a basis for management of sustainable tourism and biodiversity:

(a) Baseline information and review;

(b) Vision and goals;

(c) Objectives based on vision and goals;

(d) Review of legislation and control measures;

(e) Impact assessment;

(f) Impact management;

(g) Decision making;

(h) Implementation;

(i) Monitoring control and surveillance;

(j) Adaptive management.

The focus of each management step, and its relationship to the Convention on Biological Diversity is set out in the following table:

Management step	Focus of each management step
1.Baseline information and review	Current biodiversity and trends; current development and trends (socio-economic issues, etc.); current tourism and trends) including cost-benefit assessment (ie. internalisation of environmental and other costs re- tourism and biodiversity)
2. Vision and goals	Biodiversity, tourism, sustainable development
3. Objectives	Based on vision and goals
4. Review of legislation and control measures	Laws, regulations, standards, economic measures, effectiveness, and enforcement for biodiversity, sustainable development, and tourism
5. Impact assessment	Environmental and social impacts, including tourism effects on biodiversity - taking into account the effects of other sectors also on biodiversity and cumulative effects
6. Impact management	Potential impact management measures to address environmental and social impacts
7. Decision making	
8. Implementation	
9. Monitoring control and surveillance	Compliance with planning and biodiversity management / impact management requirements; biodiversity and changes; development and changes (socio-economic issues, etc.); tourism and changes
10. Adaptive management	Management of tourism , resources, and role and involvement of host community, with adjustment of management requirements / tourism levels in accordance with objectives for biodiversity

The assessments of tourism and biodiversity that have been carried out under the Convention on Biological Diversity, the Commission on Sustainable Development, and by various other organizations at international level, and including the private sector, conclude that:

(a) Biological diversity is a major foundation for many tourist activities;

(b) Tourism has an impact on biological diversity;

(c) Tourism can help to conserve biological diversity and to use it sustainably.

Based on internationally-agreed principles, codes, etc. on sustainable tourism and on biodiversity, the following conclusions can be drawn:

(a) All tourism should be sustainable;

(b) Management of tourism is a shared responsibility which requires the cooperation and participation of a range of different stakeholder groups;

(c) Tourism should respect local populations and the cultural specificities of host communities, and support social cohesion. This must include acknowledging the rights of indigenous and local communities to decide about, and to be fully informed prior to, tourism development, and to be active participants in the development and operation of tourism activities in their communities, lands and territories;

(d) The tourism industry acknowledges the need for travel and tourism enterprises to respect international agreements on protection of the environment. The tourism industry must be responsible for direct impacts resulting from tourism activities on the environment, including those impacts that are manifest outside of destinations but which are linked to tourism;

(e) Management of all tourism must be consistent with ecosystem processes/ ecosystem principle/ associated ecosystems etc. And must maintain and enhance ecosystem functioning and biodiversity;

(f) Tourism should protect the natural and cultural heritage, and restore damage to this heritage where this has resulted from tourism;

(g) Tourism development must be fully integrated into overall sustainable spatial development, contribute to meeting local development objectives and create steady and fairly paid employment;

(h) Tourism activities in protected areas and identified vulnerable areas should be consistent with the purposes for which those areas have been established

(i) Guiding principles relevant to sustainable tourism and to biodiversity conservation and sustainable use, have been agreed internationally - a key task now is to focus on implementation that puts these principles into practice, and in particular, to provide technical guidance to tourism managers and to biodiversity managers on ways of working together with key stakeholders to deliver:

  (i) Conservation of ecosystem structure and functioning;

  (ii) Sustainable tourism in ecosystems conserving their structure and functioning;

  (iii) Fair and equitable sharing of benefits;

  (iv) Information and capacity building;

  (v) Restoration of past damage;

(j) International guidelines are needed that provide a fully integrated approach to the general management of sustainable tourism and biodiversity, and which address the technical issues of implementation of internationally-agreed principles relevant to these areas.

3

Cultural Tourism Management

Cultural tourism is generally defined as visits by persons from outside the host community motivated wholly or in part by interest in the historical, artistic, scientific or lifestyle/heritage offerings of a community, region, group or institution. From this definition, it can be seen that cultural tourism activities may encompass many different types of experiences. While many of those can be categorized narrowly to include such activities as visiting historic sites, mueums or galleries, and attending performing arts events, they can also include aspects of other streams of tourism activity, such as "eco-tourism", "edu-tourism", "heritage-tourism", "adventure-tourism" and "agro-tourism". Indeed, cultural tourism can also include such activities as shopping, dining, and similar means of experiencing a community's culture.

Cultural tourism is a phenomeon that has gained wide currency in recent decades. A product of demographic, social and cultural trends, cultural tourism has been identified as a growing and lucrative sector of the tourism industry. Individual organizations and communities have also embraced cultural tourism as a potential economic saviour: as traditional mass employment industries continue to downsize, cities and towns have turned to cultural tourism as a particularly "21st century" generator of economic activity and jobs.

Yet there are risks involved as well — environmental degradation, strain on local infrastructure, and the so-called "Disneyfication" or commodification of treasured cultural resources are some of the potential side effects of increased numbers of tourists to a particular destination.

The growth of cultural tourism as an economic force is undeniable. Tourists looking for unique and authentic experiences are increasingly interested in cultural sites and innovative arts programming, and will travel to find these attractions.

Cultural tourism is centred around arts events, festivals, museums, art galleries, and heritage attractions is big business. Cultural tourists are increasingly drawn from the 55+ age category, earn and spend more money, spend more time in an area while vacationing, are likely to stay in hotels and motels, and are far more likely to shop. Major museum events, such as special one-time exhibitions, are tremendous tourism boosters, while annual events generate repeat visitors who plan their vacations in advance to attend the event.

Visitors drawn to a location for a specific cultural activity or event will stay longer to take advantage of other recreational activities, such as camping, hiking, skiing, and trail riding, spending even more in the local economy and the surrounding region. All sizes of communities benefit from efforts to cultivate and develop cultural offerings for visitors.

Properly managed, the tourism and travel industry can bring substantial benefits on both a macro- and local level. By providing new employment opportunities, tourism can help alleviate poverty and curb the out-migration of youth and other marginally-employed community members. Also, through bringing revenue to sites, tourism has the potential to enhance and safeguard heritage. Similarly, the much-needed foreign currency and investment that tourism brings has the power to revitalise traditional building and craft industries. On a more human level, by bringing in revenue tourism has the capacity to strengthen local people's self-respect, values and identity, thereby safeguarding aspects of their intangible heritage and enhancing their development potential.

Tourism has the power to generate both positive and negative effects. It has been described as 'a goose that not only lays a golden egg, but also fouls its own nest.' So, while tourism has the potential to enhance and preserve the tangible and intangible cultural heritage on which it relies, if it is not managed and controlled, it can also degrade and irreversibly damage this very same valuable resource. There are countless examples of how unplanned tourism, although potentially profitable in the short term, has damaged fragile historical and cultural resources, thereby undermining their value. In the same way, unplanned tourism can erode a community's self-image and cultural values, as well. Although tourism is increasingly recognised as a potentially powerful development tool, situations frequently arise where local communities are side-lined and benefit little from the tourism in their area.

Whilst these potential negative impacts of the tourism industry pose a particular threat to developing countries, avoiding these eventualities is very much a global responsibility. Indeed, the pitfalls of unplanned tourism have repeatedly arisen due to a lack of understanding of the issues involved, as well as to a lack of co-operation by parties involved at the local level - the stakeholders. Fortunately, there has been an increase in awareness among local communities, heritage conservationists and the tourism industry, alike. Increasingly, these stakeholder groups have sought advice from UNESCO and other bodies to develop models and workable solutions through which sustainable cultural tourism can be encouraged and managed. In addition, steps have been taken to design better government policies and strategies to sustainably develop heritage resources and tourism.

In this regard, the Asian Development Bank (ADB) and UNESCO convened the roundtable, Sustainable Development of Cultural Heritage and Cultural Tourism in South Asia, in New Delhi, India on 16 January 2005. The objectives of the roundtable were to:

(i) strengthen sub-regional and inter-sectoral cooperation dialogue by bringing together representatives from Ministries of Tourism, Ministries of Culture, and related private sector organizations; and

(ii) identify issues and opportunities for sub-regional cooperation in the areas of sustainable tourism development within the framework of the ADB SASEC Tourism Development Plan (TDP) and the UNESCO regional Buddhist heritage revival project.

During the meeting, participants divided into three sub-groups to discuss and identify platforms for collaboration. The three sub-groups reflected three tiers of human resource development and capacity-building, as follows:

(i) Local Empowerment;

(ii) Knowledge Resources; and

(iii) Policies for Coordination between Tourism and Heritage Development.

Each sub-group was asked to map stakeholders and to identify current problems, institutional platforms needed for ensuring collaboration between tourism and heritage development, and specific activities linked with TDP priorities, including human resource development projects. The Roundtable participants suggested a range of strategies for identifying priority pilot projects, and made four main recommendations, as outlined below.

> "In response to the existing situation at heritage sites, characterized by limited involvement in decision-making by local stakeholders and a lack of understanding between various layers of stakeholders, the first recommendation was that management committees should be formed at key heritage sites in order to provide a forum for dialogue. The second recommendation was that education and skills in management, business enterprise and sustainable development should be provided to enable equitable and informed participation by stakeholders in this forum. In addition to improving understanding between groups, such an educational framework would lead to better promotion, marketing and management of heritage tourism sites by raising awareness of the links between conservation and tourism among both tourists and local residents.
>
> Recognizing the lack of information-sharing between those involved in cultural tourism and cultural heritage, the third recommendation was that cross-sectoral mentoring/training programmes be established, including training in management skills, so as to increase understanding between the two fields and improve service provision and resource management.
>
> Given the ad hoc and inappropriate provision of social/physical infrastructure, services and skills development, the fourth recommendation was that governments work towards strengthening institutional platforms and raising awareness about the importance of cultural assets. By strengthening institutional platforms and providing options for sustainably developing cultural assets, coordination between agencies would be enhanced, policy planning improved and clear work management plans developed, thereby ensuring better management of heritage tourism sites and the optimal use of resources."

Cultural Resources Management (CRM)

Cultural resources management (CRM) is a branch of archaeology concerned with the identification, maintenance, and preservation of significant cultural sites in the face of threats such as development, erosion or unsustainable visitor numbers. It also stresses the importance of heritage interpretation and presentation in communicating the value of heritage to government and the public.

It has its roots in the rescue archaeology and urban archaeology undertaken throughout North America and Europe in the years surrounding World War II and the succeeding decades. Salvage projects were hasty attempts to identify and rescue archaeological remains before they were destroyed to make room for large public-works projects or other construction. In the early days of salvage archaeology, it was nearly unheard-of for a project to be delayed because of the presence of even the most fascinating cultural sites, so it behooved the salvage archaeologists to work as fast as possible. Although many sites were lost, much data was saved for posterity through these salvage efforts.

In more recent decades, legislation has been passed that emphasizes the identification and protection of cultural sites, especially those on public lands. In the United States, the most notable of these laws remains the National Historic Preservation Act. The administration of President Richard Nixon was most instrumental in passing and developing this legislation, although it has been extended and elaborated upon since. These laws make it a crime to develop any federal lands without conducting a cultural resources survey in order to identify and assess any cultural sites that may be impacted. In the United Kingdom, PPG 16 has been instrumental in improving the management of historic sites in the face of development.

CRM Techniques

While archaeological sites remain the primary focus for most CRM archaologists, other work such as ethnohistorical projects and public outreach also fall within their purview. A phase of evaluation is considered important in assessing the significance of a threatened site. This can comprise a desk-based study, a wide area survey or trial trenching.

If no significant archaeological sites are found in the impacted area, construction may proceed as planned. If potentially significant remains are found, construction may be delayed to allow for excavation and evaluation of the site or sites found within the impacted area. This is done to determine the archaeological site's true significants. If archaeologists determine the site contains important/significant cultural remains, the adverse effects on the site must be mitigated.

Site mitigation can involve avoidance of the site, or having a percentage of the site being excavated to recover the data. These restrictions involve any federal project involving the possible distrubance of culutral resources, and can extend to state and private development efforts as well, if those efforts involve public waterways or federal funds.

If archaeologists determine the site contains highly significant cultural remains, the adverse development effects on the site must be mitigated through a structured programme that is often long and expensive. Alternatively an important site may be designated as being protected by the state so that no development at all can take place. In the United Kingdom, all forms of development, public and private are subject to archaeological requirements whilst in the United States, this work can only be undertaken in Federally-funded projects or those on government-owned land.

Eeffect of CRM

CRM has been a mixed blessing for archaeology. Preservation legislation has ensured that no valuable site will be destroyed by construction without study, but the work of CRM archaeologists is not always sound. Some academic archaeologists do not take CRM work seriously, because of its emphasis on site identification and preservation rather than intensive study and analysis. CRM firms obtain contracts through a bidding process; it is not unusual for the company responsible for construction to select the bid with the lowest price estimate, regardless of the soundness of the submitted plan, though this not always the case. The impact of CRM has been considerable; given the large amount of construction, the bulk of archaeological work in the United States and the United Kingdom is conducted through CRM channels.

Management of Cultural Heritage

Cultural heritage is the value people have given to items and places through their association with those items and places. These values include those of significance to Aboriginal people, places of social value to the community, and places of historic, architectural or scientific significance, and therefore encompass both Aboriginal and historic heritage.While cultural heritage is often spoken about as either Aboriginal or historic (non-Aboriginal), this distinction is misleading because all members of the community have had a shared history within the landscape. For example, Aboriginal cultural heritage has associations in pastoral landscapes as well as associations linked with the mission period. This notion represents a shift in conventional cultural heritage management, and acknowledges that culture belongs as much in the present as it does in the past and that it evolves and changes along with society.

All landscapes contain cultural heritage. People assign values to those landscapes including those associated with knowledge, songs, stories, art, objects, places, events, buildings, dreaming paths and/or human remains. In addition, natural elements of the landscape that acquire meaning for a particular Aboriginal group are considered to have cultural heritage value, and may include landforms, minerals and biodiversity. Cultural heritage also represents the continuity from one generation to another of a group's culture, values and attitudes.

There has been a shift in the approach of park management organisations, to move from a focus on cultural heritage management of objects and sites to the more inclusive definition of cultural heritage described above. It is a move from limiting the assessment of the significance of cultural heritage to scientific methods such as archaeology, to including the assessment of social significance. This approach involves communities in providing their explanation of why something is of cultural and social importance to them.

Objectives for Cultural Heritage Management

The primary objectives for cultural heritage management are to:

- acknowledge the intrinsic link between Aboriginal cultural heritage and the natural environment
- manage Aboriginal and historic heritage places, landscapes, cultural practices and stories on park
- manage evidence of past land uses such as agriculture or mining in addition to specific significant historic places and landscapes, and reflect shared histories between the Aboriginal and non-Aboriginal people that worked together in these industries

— present and interpret significant cultural heritage places to park users and visitors

— work actively with community groups to facilitate the conservation of and access to their heritage, including the provision of access to parks to continue cultural practices

— facilitate conservation outcomes through the sustainable use of buildings, landscapes and places, thus enabling a vibrant and living approach to heritage conservation and management.

Assessing Significance

Interpreting the cultural significance of places and landscapes is based on an analysis of oral, documentary and physical evidence, and their social, aesthetic, historic and scientific values. Working closely with the relevant communities is essential to fully understand cultural heritage and so develop more effective conservation outcomes.

Producing a plan of management is the first stage in assessing the significance of the cultural heritage within a park. This enables park managers to consider whether key values require more detailed assessments. Statements of significance (SoS) are prepared for high priority historic cultural heritage within parks. A SoS also makes general recommendations about the most appropriate method of management such as protection from pests and weeds or vandalism, or may involve more active management. If the site is highly significant or the management of the site is likely to be complex, a conservation management plan (CMP) may be prepared.

Underpinning the assessment of the significance of cultural heritage is a program of strategic research. The key themes presently being investigated include cultural landscapes, the integration of natural and cultural heritage conservation, social significance, cross cultural studies, women's heritage, and neighbours and communities.

Planning for Management

Where the significance of historic heritage has been assessed and further planning is required, a CMP is produced. A CMP outlines the values of a place in detail, describes their significance and associated history, then sets out the actions required for proper management of the place, for both restoring it to an acceptable standard and for cyclical maintenance. The development of CMPs is supported by a range of guidelines and standards to assist park managers in planning for the appropriate management and protection of cultural heritage.

The cultural heritage management strategies also help determine the long-term conservation and management outcomes that CMPs should aim to achieve. Included in a CMP, where appropriate, are options for education and interpretation of a site for park visitors.

Management Programs

There are a range of ways in which cultural heritage is managed within parks. Recommendations for management are made through a statement of significance or a CMP for high priority or highly significant cultural heritage. The type of management that may be required ranges from stabilisation works, protective fencing, emergency or conservation works, installing interpretive signage or threat mitigation works.When active works are required for a site, park managers may first be required to undertake a Review of Environmental Factors (REF) or an Environmental Impact Statement (EIS) to consider the impact of the works on both natural and cultural values. The cost of restoration and maintenance of all the built heritage on parks exceeds the funding available, so careful targeting is necessary.

Management may involve providing appropriate interpretation and education — for the benefit of the wider community — about the significance of the place to aboriginal communities. Discovery programs, publications and interpretive material all communicate the importance of cultural heritage to the community.

Managing cultural heritage requires specialist skills and knowledge such as those necessary to protect and conserve Aboriginal rock art sites. To assist in training new park staff and land managers from other organisations a field-based training program and accompanying guidelines that aim to reduce a range of pressures on the integrity of rock art sites should be developed. These include natural pressures such as water damage (mitigated through the use of silicon) or accumulation of lichen or mud from nest-building insects (carefully removed using special techniques), and unnatural pressures such as damage caused by livestock (managed through pest control, fencing or the use of cattle grids). Additional subjects currently being prepared include site monitoring techniques and ways of managing sites for visitation, including dealing with vandalism and graffiti.

Archaeology is also a specialist skill and can contribute appreciably to our understanding of how people lived in the past, an essential part of cultural heritage. Archaeology has provided important information about the lives of Aboriginal and non-Aboriginal people through the discovery of artefacts, structural remains and other items, revealing how previous generations lived and the complex exchanges and interconnections between Aboriginal and non-Aboriginal people. This provides us with a unique insight into the dynamics of exchange between cultures during periods where historical records alone do not provide a complete picture. Other important tools for preserving cultural heritage are historical research and oral history projects.

Revised Plan of Action for International Co-operation on Tourism Management in Heritage Cities

The participants to the 2nd International Seminar on "Tourism Management in Heritage Cities", held in Nazareth, Israel, 3-5 February 2000, agreed to adopt the following Plan of Action for the Network activities in the years 2000-2001:

1. Appreciating the important results of the Project "Art Cities and Visitors Flow" launched in 1991 by the University of Venice and the UNESCO Venice Office - Regional Office for Science and Technology in Europe (UVO-ROSTE), which presented new perspectives and strategies for tourist flow management in art cities in Europe and led to the establishment of a network of art cities in Europe;
2. Appreciating also the launch of "Network on Tourism Management in Heritage Cities in Europe and the Mediterranean" launched at its Preparatory Seminar held in Venice from 18 to 19 December 1998, which extends a network of art cities to Heritage Cities in general,
3. Emphasising that the objective of new Network is to advance knowledge of the management of tourism in heritage cities in Europe and the Mediterranean and enhance its sharing through different activities as well as by means of information technology,

4. Underlining that the new Network of Heritage Cities in Europe and the Mediterranean should be an open-ended network for international co-operation, and that it should systematically look for connection with existing similar initiatives, namely by international organisations,

5. Recognising that, in the situation of heritage cities, sustainable tourism development is closely related to the sustainable development of heritage cities, and therefore it becomes a priority for local authorities to formulate and implement proper cultural tourism policy in partnership with private sector, and with the participation of citizens,

6. Noting also that the right balance should be stroke between the issue of valorising of the heritage as a means to generate both welfare opportunities for the host community – which bears the costs of tourist exploitation – and the financial means needed to preserve and promote the heritage itself; and the imperative of conservation of the physical integrity, value, and symbols embodied in the heritage for the future generations and the collective memory,

7. Approving, with positive evaluation, of the reports of the activities carried out through the Network in 1998 and 1999 presented at the 2nd International Seminar,

Recommend toPpromote the Following Initiatives for the Years 2000-2001:

1. International co-operation on the following emerging issues, in collaboration with local, national, and international institutions:
   — The design and implementation of advanced systems of visitor flow management;

— The formulation and implementation of "wise" policies for sustainable urban tourism, that is, respectful of heritage and local communities;

— The identification of innovative public actions involving and empowering stakeholders at different levels – through inter-sectoral co-operation and public-private partnerships – ensuring them a proper formation so that economic viability and community vision to the participated approach to policymaking for sustainable development is guaranteed;

— The enhancement of the participation of local communities in the decision-making process as well as the democratic access to cultural resources and facilities;

— The systematic establishment of co-operative relations with representatives of the tourism industry, as a means to strengthen the effectiveness and comprehensiveness of policymaking for sustainable tourism at the local and global level;

— The organisation of training and education in the management of cultural tourism in the existing and perspective segments of employment and administration;

— The innovative use of new information technologies for the purpose managing effectively both heritage conservation and tourism development.

2. Individual and bi-lateral projects on the above issues, facilitating personnel exchange and training, and mutual knowledge sharing;
3. A workshop (to be held in a selected city in the year 2001), on the related topics of the Network;

4. An International Conference (to be held during the first half of the year 2002 in the city of Bruges, Cultural Capital of Europe for that year), to evaluate the results of activities to be carried out in the period 1999-2002 for further advancement of the Network;
5. The publication of an authoritative manual entitled "Guidelines for Tourism Management in Heritage Cities" in co-operation with several partners including, among others, the Aliance des Villes Européennes de Culture (AVEC), WTO, ICOMOS, with the aim of providing comprehensive orientations to tourism managers in the field of cultural tourism, together with general principles for sustainable tourism management supported by specific cases and experiences;
6. Further promotion of the UNESCO World Heritage Convention in order to enhance the widespread understanding of – and support to – heritage preservation and enhancement;

Moreover, the participants recommend that the following long-term activities in terms of the management and promotion of the network activities;

7. The extension of the Network website;
8. Active efforts to ensure the contribution of the mass-media in promoting the objectives and undertakings of the Network to the general public;
9. The enhanced diffusion of information on the Network through the networks of universities and research centres affiliated with UNESCO so as to ensure the appropriate technical and scientific support to the Network;
10. Effective management of the Network by a steering committee to be established, under the co-ordination

of UVO and UNESCO in Paris, in partnership with international institutions, universities, NGOs, city authorities, and the tourism industry, as well as existing networks concerned.

International Cultural Tourism Charter Managing Tourism at Places of Heritage Significance

(8th Draft, for Adoption by ICOMOS at the 12th General Assembly, Mexico, October 1999)

The Charter Ethos

At the broadest level, the natural and cultural heritage belongs to all people. We each have a right and responsibility to understand, appreciate and conserve its universal values.

Heritage is a broad concept and includes the natural as well as the cultural environment. It encompasses landscapes, historic places, sites and built environments, as well as biodiversity, collections, past and continuing cultural practices, knowledge and living experiences. It records and expresses the long processes of historic development, forming the essence of diverse national, regional, indigenous and local identities and is an integral part of modern life. It is a dynamic reference point and positive instrument for growth and change. The particular heritage and collective memory of each locality or community is irreplaceable and an important foundation for development, both now and into the future.

At a time of increasing globalisation, the protection, conservation, interpretation and presentation of the heritage and cultural diversity of any particular place or region is an important challenge for people everywhere. However, management of that heritage, within a framework of internationally recognised and appropriately applied standards, is usually the responsibility of the particular community or custodian group.

A primary objective for managing heritage is to communicate its significance and need for its conservation to its host community and to visitors. Reasonable and well managed physical, intellectual and/ or emotive access to heritage and cultural development is both a right and a privilege. It brings with it a duty of respect for the heritage values, interests and equity of the present-day host community, indigenous custodians or owners of historic property and for the landscapes and cultures from which that heritage evolved.

The Dynamic Interaction between Tourism and Cultural Heritage

Domestic and international tourism continues to be among the foremost vehicles for cultural exchange, providing a personal experience, not only of that which has survived from the past, but of the contemporary life and society of others. It is increasingly appreciated as a positive force for natural and cultural conservation. Tourism can capture the economic characteristics of the heritage and harness these for conservation by generating funding, educating the community and influencing policy. It is an essential part of many national and regional economies and can be an important factor in development, when managed successfully.

Tourism itself has become an increasingly complex phenomenon, with political, economic, social, cultural, educational, bio-physical, ecological and aesthetic dimensions. The achievement of a beneficial inter-action between the potentially conflicting expectations and aspirations of visitors and host or local communities, presents many challenges and opportunities.

The natural and cultural heritage, diversities and living cultures are major tourism attractions. Excessive or poorly-managed tourism and tourism related development can threaten their physical nature, integrity and significant characteristics. The ecological setting, culture and lifestyles of host communities may also be degraded, along with the visitor's experience of the place.

Tourism should bring benefits to host communities and provide an important means and motivation for them to care for and maintain their heritage and cultural practices. The involvement and co-operation of local and/or indigenous community representatives, conservationists, tourism operators, property owners, policy makers, those preparing national development plans and site managers is necessary to achieve a sustainable tourism industry and enhance the protection of heritage resources for future generations.

ICOMOS, the International Council on Monuments and Sites, as the author of this Charter, other international organisations and the tourism industry, are dedicated to this challenge.

Objectives of the Charter

The Objectives of the International Cultural Tourism Charter are:

— To facilitate and encourage those involved with heritage conservation and management to make the significance of that heritage accessible to the host community and visitors.

— To facilitate and encourage the tourism industry to promote and manage tourism in ways that respect and enhance the heritage and living cultures of host communities.

— To facilitate and encourage a dialogue between conservation interests and the tourism industry about the importance and fragile nature of heritage places, collections and living cultures including the need to achieve a sustainable future for them.

— To encourage those formulating plans and policies to develop detailed, measurable goals and strategies relating to the presentation and interpretation of heritage places and cultural activities, in the context of their preservation and conservation.

In addition,

— The Charter supports wider initiatives by ICOMOS, other international bodies and the tourism industry in maintaining the integrity of heritage management and conservation.

— The Charter encourages the involvement of all those with relevant or at times conflicting interests, responsibilities and obligations to join in achieving its objectives.

— The Charter encourages the formulation of detailed guidelines by interested parties, facilitating the implementation of the Principles to their specific circumstances or the requirements of particular organisations and communities.

Principles of the Cultural Tourism Charter

Principle 1

Since domestic and international tourism is among the foremost vehicles for cultural exchange, conservation should provide responsible and well managed opportunities for members of the host community and visitors to experience and understand that community's heritage and culture at first hand.

1.1. The natural and cultural heritage is a material and spiritual resource, providing a narrative of historical development. It has an important role in modern life and should be made physically, intellectually and/or emotively accessible to the general public. Programmes for the protection and conservation of the physical attributes, intangible aspects, contemporary cultural expressions and broad context, should facilitate an understanding and appreciation of the heritage significance by the host community and the visitor, in an equitable and affordable manner.

1.2. Individual aspects of natural and cultural heritage have differing levels of significance, some with universal values, others of national, regional or local importance. Interpretation programmes should present that significance in a relevant and accessible manner to the host community and the visitor, with appropriate, stimulating and contemporary forms of education, media, technology and personal explanation of historical, environmental and cultural information.

1.3. Interpretation and presentation programmes should facilitate and encourage the high level of public awareness and support necessary for the long term survival of the natural and cultural heritage.

1.4. Interpretation programmes should present the significance of heritage places, traditions and cultural practices within the past experience and present diversities of the area and the host community, including that of minority cultural or linguistic groups. The visitor should always be informed of the differing cultural values that may be ascribed to a particular heritage resource.

Principle 2

The relationship between Heritage Places and Tourism is

dynamic and may involve conflicting values. It should be managed in a sustainable way for present and future generations.

2.1. Places of heritage significance have an intrinsic value for all people as an important basis for cultural diversity and social development. The long term protection and conservation of living cultures, heritage places, collections, their physical and ecological integrity and their environmental context, should be an essential component of social, economic, political, legislative, cultural and tourism development policies.

2.2. The interaction between heritage resources or values and tourism is dynamic and ever changing, generating both opportunities and challenges, as well as potential conflicts. Tourism projects, activities and developments should achieve positive outcomes and minimise adverse impacts on the heritage and lifestyles of the host community, while responding to the needs and aspirations of the visitor.

2.3. Conservation, interpretation and tourism development programmes should be based on a comprehensive understanding of the specific, but often complex or conflicting aspects of heritage significance of the particular place. Continuing research and consultation are important to furthering the evolving understanding and appreciation of that significance.

2.4. The retention of the authenticity of heritage places and collections is important. It is an essential element of their cultural significance, as expressed in the physical material, collected memory and intangible traditions that remain from the past. Programmes should present and interpret the authenticity of places and cultural experiences to enhance the appreciation and understanding of that cultural heritage.

2.5. Tourism development and infrastructure projects should take account of the aesthetic, social and cultural dimensions, natural and cultural landscapes, bio-diversity characteristics and the broader visual context of heritage places. Preference should be given to using local materials and take account of local architectural styles or vernacular traditions.

2.6. Before heritage places are promoted or developed for increased tourism, management plans should assess the natural and cultural values of the resource. They should then establish appropriate limits of acceptable change, particularly in relation to the impact of visitor numbers on the physical characteristics, integrity, ecology and biodiversity of the place, local access and transportation systems and the social, economic and cultural well being of the host community. If the likely level of change is unacceptable the development proposal should be modified.

2.7. There should be on-going programmes of evaluation to assess the progressive impacts of tourism activities and development on the particular place or community.

Principle 3

Conservation and Tourism Planning for Heritage Places should ensure that the Visitor Experience will be worthwhile, satisfying and enjoyable.

3.1. Conservation and tourism programmes should present high quality information to optimise the visitor's understanding of the significant heritage characteristics and of the need for their protection, enabling the visitor to enjoy the place in an appropriate manner.

3.2. Visitors should be able to experience the heritage place at their own pace, if they so choose. Specific circulation routes may be necessary to minimise impacts on the integrity and physical fabric of a place, its natural and cultural characteristics.

3.3. Respect for the sanctity of spiritual places, practices and traditions is an important consideration for site managers, visitors, policy makers, planners and tourism operators. Visitors should be encouraged to behave as welcomed guests, respecting the values and lifestyles of the host community, rejecting possible theft or illicit trade in cultural property and conducting themselves in a responsible manner which would generate a renewed welcome, should they return.

3.4. Planning for tourism activities should provide appropriate facilities for the comfort, safety and well being of the visitor, that enhance the enjoyment of the visit but do not adversely impact on the significant features or ecological characteristics.

Principle 4

Host communities and indigenous peoples should be involved in planning for conservation and tourism.

4.1. The rights and interests of the host community, at regional and local levels, property owners and relevant indigenous peoples who may exercise traditional rights or responsibilities over their own land and its significant sites, should be respected. They should be involved in establishing goals, strategies, policies and protocols for the identification, conservation, management, presentation and interpretation of their heritage resources, cultural practices and contemporary cultural expressions, in the tourism context.

4.2. While the heritage of any specific place or region may have a universal dimension, the needs and wishes of some communities or indigenous peoples to restrict or manage physical, spiritual or intellectual access to certain cultural practices, knowledge, beliefs, activities, artefacts or sites should be respected.

Principle 5

Tourism and conservation activities should benefit the host community.

5.1. Policy makers should promote measures for the equitable distribution of the benefits of tourism to be shared across countries or regions, improving the levels of socio-economic development and contributing where necessary to poverty alleviation.

5.2. Conservation management and tourism activities should provide equitable economic, social and cultural benefits to the men and women of the host or local community, at all levels, through education, training and the creation of full time employment opportunities.

5.3. A significant proportion of the revenue specifically derived from tourism programmes to heritage places should be allotted to the protection, conservation and presentation of those places, including their natural and cultural contexts. Where possible, visitors should be advised of this revenue allocation.

5.4. Tourism programmes should encourage the training and employment of guides and site interpreters from the host community to enhance the skills of local people in the presentation and interpretation of their cultural values.

5.5. Heritage interpretation and education programmes among the people of the host community should encourage the involvement of local site interpreters. The programmes should promote a knowledge and respect for their heritage, encouraging the local people to take a direct interest in its care and conservation.

5.6. Conservation management and tourism programmes should include education and training opportunities for policy makers, planners, researchers, designers, architects, interpreters, conservators and tourism operators. Participants should be encouraged to understand and help resolve the at times conflicting issues, opportunities and problems encountered by their colleagues.

Principle 6

Tourism promotion programmes should protect and enhance Natural and Cultural Heritage characteristics.

6.1. Tourism promotion programmes should create realistic expectations and responsibly inform potential visitors of the specific heritage characteristics of a place or host community, thereby encouraging them to behave appropriately.

6.2. Places and collections of heritage significance should be promoted and managed in ways which protect their authenticity and enhance the visitor experience by minimising fluctuations in arrivals and avoiding excessive numbers of visitors at any one time.

6.3. Tourism promotion programmes should provide a wider distribution of benefits and relieve the pressures on more popular places by encouraging visitors to experience the wider cultural and natural heritage characteristics of the region or locality.

6.4. The promotion, distribution and sale of local crafts and other products should provide a reasonable social and economic return to the host community, while ensuring that their cultural integrity is not degraded.

4

Management of Wildlife-based Recreational Activities

Tourism continues to be recognised as the fastest growing industry in the world. According to the World Tourism Organisation WTO, world tourism grew by an estimated 7.4 percent in 2000, its highest growth rate in nearly a decade, and almost doubled the increase of 1999. In today's global environment, the management and sustainable utilisation of natural resources is a major challenge facing Governments and their national economies. In this regard, countries all over the world, have placed a premium on such resources and have implemented a number of measures to ensure sustainable utilisation. Wildlife is among these resources, and its effective management has attracted international tourists, thereby making tourism one of the major foreign exchange earners for the country and an important socioeconomic growth sector.

Wildlife has been recognized as one of the three main valuable natural resources, alongside minerals and rangelands. It contributes to the cultural, socio-economic and biological integrity of the country. Furthermore, benefits from wildlife are the creation of economic opportunities and diversification with potential for sustainable development; it enhances environmental stability and contributes to tourism development; and provides aesthetic, scientific, nutritional and educational values.

The regional and global environment within which government operates is changing rapidly and becoming much more competitive. Domestically, the wildlife sector is competing for limited human and financial resources with other equally deserving sectors. As a result, there is need to improve efficiency of Wildlife and National Parks to ensure it gives value for money. The globalisation of wildlife conservation issues requires that great care be exercised in making decisions that affect the management of wildlife resources. Greater efforts will be made and measures put in place to reduce the land use conflict relating to humans and wildlife.

Human-Wildlife Conflict

Conflicts between humans and wildlife continue to be a major source of controversy between those who suffer damage and the government. Damage caused by wildlife to livestock, crops and other properties, and the inadequate or lack of compensation for such damage has always caused consternation among rural populations. However, it should be noted that man and wildlife have co-existed since time immemorial and so has the problem.

Most of the conflicts arise from the fact that livestock areas have encroached into wildlife areas to the extent that some livestock areas are only a few hundred meters from the wildlife areas. Farming methods, especially the protection of crops and livestock, need to be improved to help minimise the conflicts.

In order to sustain wildlife populations, efforts will be made to minimize human/wildlife conflicts by working with the relevant authorities to deter livestock from encroaching into wildlife areas and wildlife from causing damage to people's property. A better balance will be struck between the needs of wildlife and that of humans in order for to sustain wildlife populations into the future. More specifically, the following actions are being or will be taken to address the conflict between humans, livestock and wildlife:

a. Fencing projects.

b. Increase of problem animal control manpower and opening up new stations/camps.

c. Provision of equipment and boreholes.

The intervention of man in the ecosystem directly puts him in competition with wildlife for various amenities including space, water, and vegetation, whereupon at times human life has been threatened. Man has expanded and driven animals further into small pockets. Every time a game animal tries to fend for itself, it directly or indirectly conflicts with the interest of man. Predators that come from protected areas and wander into cattle posts kill livestock.

Equally, livestock wander into protected areas and compete with wildlife for grazing and water resources. Wildlife which come into contact with livestock is sometimes also blamed for diseases affecting domestic animals as in the case of foot and mouth, anthrax and rabies, to name a few. Similarly, this contact with domestic animals can result in disease transmission to wildlife, which is potentially fatal, particularly in the case of predators. Examples of such diseases are rabies, canine distemper, etc.

Demands of Wildlife-based Enterprises

Management of forests for recreation and wildlifebased enterprises has the potential to benefit both private forest owners and rural residents in general. Such recreational activities such as camping, horseback riding, cross-country skiing, spelunking, touring historic or archeological sites, rafting, and mountain biking offer possible supplemental income opportunities. Both consumptive and nonconsumptive wildlife-based enterprises can be developed for commercial hunting, fishing, and appreciative use activities such as wildlife observation, bird watching, photography, the informal or formal field education of schoolchildren and adults, and even basic and applied scientific research.

Developing recreation-based enterprises or charging for recreational access will not be a solution for all forest landowners. Entrepreneurs must have a thorough and objective understanding of the characteristics, merits, and potential pitfalls of these enterprises before making an investment decision.

The overall demand for recreation continues to grow, although not as rapidly as it did in the 1960's and 1970's. Societal trends have a strong impact on recreation, and in the United States entrepreneurs should be advised that there are strong indications that past patterns are shifting. The "baby boom" generation that first flooded schools and colleges, then the labor force, and then the housing market is now in its forties.

These are typically the most productive (and demanding) years of life. At the same time, the median workweek length has been increasing, a higher percentage of women are in the work force, and people are approaching a period of economic restraint to make up for the massive debts incurred at the Federal level. All of these trends imply some important changes in demand for recreation services in our society.

In the future, recreational activities are likely to become more planned and deliberate because an older, more highly educated public will become more selective in their purchases. For the same reason, the quality of the recreational experience, including level of maintenance, aesthetics, and safety, will rise in importance. Shorter but more frequent trips nearer to home are likely to be the rule. Demand for vigorous physical activities is high and is expected to remain strong in the near future. A continued increase in interest in exercise will also lead to increased demand for close-to-home opportunities for bicycling, jogging, walking, and observing nature.

Managing Hunting and Fishing Operations

Hunting is still a popular sport, but participation rates for hunting have been declining over time. The total number of hunters is also beginning to decline. The major problem is limited access to land on which to hunt. Wildlife normally belongs to the State and cannot be sold, but landowners can sell access, assuming they abide by all state game regulations.

Many landowners have found they can charge access and/or service fees for recreational use if, through habitat maintenance and enhancement, their property can produce sustainable densities of game species, if a good recreational experience can be provided to the hunter, and if access can be controlled. The resource base need not all be on private land, either. A relatively small property that provides access to national or state forest lands could support a hunting club.

Hunting lease operations are becoming widely accepted. The simplest type of arrangement is a basic access fee agreement, formalized with a written lease. It can provide a supplementary source of income to a landowner without large investments of time or money. Most hunting lease operations lease on an annual payment basis. However, a few enterprising landowners are leasing their properties for 5 years but are receiving payment when the lease is signed.

Through leasing, the landowner can control the number, activity, and location of recreationists on his or her property. Hunters who have paid for hunting rights have a proprietary interest in the land and are usually willing to watch for uninvited hunters, timber thieves, and other intruders. The landowner can thus gain control over property that may have been trespassed or vandalized in the past. The landowner both protects his or her property and has the security of knowing exactly who is on the land during the various hunting seasons. The user, of course, benefits from reserved, uncrowded hunting or fishing areas.

With fee hunting, the hunter usually pays on a daily basis to hunt geese, ducks, small game, deer, big game, pheasants, quail, or exotic species on a hunting preserve. A hunting preserve is land acreage either owned or leased upon which pen-reared game birds or other game animals are released over a period of 5 or more months for the purpose of sport hunting. Preserves are licensed by the State wildlife agency. The best sites for hunting preserves are farmland with some timber.

A hunting preserve may be a commercial or a noncommercial enterprise. A noncommercial hunting preserve provides quality hunting for one group of hunters on a nonprofit basis. It may be on land leased to a private coop preserve that is supported by its co-op members and operated by a group of organized sportsmen, or it may be a do-it-yourself hunting preserve. In either case, the organization needs to be incorporated and carry liability and property damage insurance. Co-op preserves usually contract with a game breeder for biweekly delivery of game.

A commercial hunting preserve is one designed to provide a profit for the owner/operator who furnishes quality hunting to those willing to pay for it. It can be open to the public on a daily fee basis or on a membership basis. Commercial preserves require both a large personal and financial commitment, although the largest financial outlay is land.

The most successful operators are those who obtain a year-round income from a combination of activities, such as boarding and training dogs, breeding game, farming, camping, fishing, picnicking, field dog trials, riflery and archery, and clay target shooting. To be profitable, each commercial operator must decide on the proper mix of activities offered, based on skills, location, and facilities. Perhaps the most important requirement is to have the financial resources to operate at a loss for at least 3 years.

Usually, along with this type of shooting preserve, there are supporting goods and services offered such as pickers, taxidermy, licenses, meals, lodging, ammunition and other shooting supplies, and sporting clays. There may also be fishing tackle, bait, boarding and training of dogs, boat rentals, and guide services, to name a few. It is also possible to combine hunting programs with other wildlife-based recreation activities that are nonconsumptive, but it requires careful management and diplomacy because of strong antihunting sentiments held by many recreationists.

Fee fishing operations offer an opportunity to supply the growing demand for sport fishing. Some entrepreneurs recommend that a small admission fee be charged with a charge per fish or per pound of fish caught . If a particular location has an area large enough to be sectioned off, a "fly fishing only, catch and release" area can be added and a fee charged for time.

Other services available at fee fishing enterprises might include bait sales, picnic and camping sites, fish cleaning, rod and reel rentals, swimming, lodging, and in some cases, boat and motor rentals. Operations near large urban centers would have the greatest potential for success. In summary, a few fishing and hunting business opportunities are as follows:

— Leasing land for hunting privileges

— Boat/motor rentals

— Hunting preserves

— Sporting clays

— Leasing water for fishing privileges

— Duck blinds

— Leasing land for trapping privileges

— Game and fish processing

— Organized hunts

— Habitat improvement

— Guide services

— Raising fish and game for stocking purposes

— Taxidermy

— Room and board for hunters and anglers

— Ammunition and fish bait

— Boarding and training of dogs

Nonconsumptive Uses of Wildlife

Most city-dwelling people who yearn for more contact with nature and look forward with great anticipation to vacation opportunities to "head for the hills" are willing to pay for access to back-to-nature experiences. However, most of them are not seeking game or fish. The fact that the majority of people enjoy wildlife without hunting has led many states to try to find ways for landowners to capture more of the economic value of wildlife viewing and similar nonconsumptive activities as important components of tourism and recreation development programs. The landowner or recreation host who can show his or her guests a variety of animals in attractive natural settings will have the advantage over those who cannot.

Nonconsumptive wildlife-related recreation means the observing, photographing, and feeding of fish and wildlife, and three out of four persons in the United States are involved in these appreciative uses. In a study done by the U.S. Fish and Wildlife Service, it was found that 47 percent of the people who took the kind of trips to natural areas for nonconsumptive activities indicated that woodlands were visited most often. For the landowner in the urban outskirts, the demand for nonconsumptive uses of wildlife could be met by providing areas for bird watching and general observations of other animals in their normal habitat. Along with this, supplies for photography, guides, and seed, etc., can be sold. A small store in the back of a barn would do just fine.

In rural areas, private farm and forest lands shelter a great variety of interesting natural resources that, if managed properly and in conjunction with other goods and services, can attract an affluent clientele interested in enjoying the beauty of forest lands. Just as bed-andbreakfast establishments advertise their existence near antique shops and historic sites and hotels provide their guests with jogging trail maps, so landowners interested in developing an appreciative clientele could offer naturalist guide services and develop trail maps of nearby habitats and lists of species that may be seen. School districts and other institutions may also pay for the privilege of bringing classes to private habitats if the quality of information services is high.

General Recreation

Other recreational enterprises that are possible in rural forest regions include campgrounds and summer camps, horse stables, swimming and fishing lakes, ski resorts, and snowmobile courses. Unfortunately, current data on the market potential and financial feasibility of these types of enterprises are largely unavailable.

Campgrounds

Many parents today are eager to share the outdoors with their children and to have time together as a family on camping vacations. Particularly in rural forested regions, campgrounds can offer an inexpensive alternative getaway experience for young families. Weekend camping is also popular, reflecting the national travel trend toward shorter, closer-to-home vacations. The camping industry has responded by providing a number of amenities that make camping more accessible and comfortable.

Today most private campgrounds offer modern plumbing, hot showers, electricity, utility hookups, and access to swimming pools and laundry facilities. Some commercial campgrounds offer miniature golf, tennis, croquet, horseshoes, fishing, boating, and even restaurants, hot tubs, and saunas. One route for entrepreneurs interested in the campground market is to enter a campground franchise.

For example, Kampground of America (KOA) currently has about 600 franchised campgrounds, including 50 in Canada and a few in Mexico. These may vary in size from 50 sites to 800 sites. KOA facilities always include a convenience store, clean rest rooms, and hot individual showers. They usually include swimming facilities, a laundry, a game room, and recreation facilities on the campground.

Many operate as a base camp and tie in with natural attractions in the area, perhaps even providing transportation to those attractions. In addition to campsites, more than 350 KOA campgrounds now also offer simple log cabins that sleep four to six individuals and rent for $20 to $30 a night. Other KOA campgrounds offer kitchen facilities with stoves, sinks, and tables.

KOA sells the rights to use the KOA logo, and belonging to the franchise gives the campground owner access to the marketing, advertising, and management expertise KOA has gained in 30 years as a camping company. The franchise provides national advertising and an annual directory. Individuals may purchase an existing KOA, build a new campground, or convert from an independent to a KOA campground. Each campground has a protected territory to prevent competition among KOA owners. While there is no evidence that well-managed franchised campgrounds are more or less profitable than wellmanaged campgrounds without a franchise name, the promotional efforts and quality guarantee of a parent company can definitely help if the basic package of facilities and services represented by the company is what the customer is seeking. This characteristic of reliability and predictability is viewed as a key to success.

However, the cost to join a franchise may be high. KOA, for example, requires payment of about $25,000 as a nonrefundable franchise fee. Costs vary depending on whether the operation is a conversion, a resale of an existing campground, or a new campground. During operation, the holder of the franchise pays the KOA company an 8 percent royalty plus a 2 percent advertising assessment based on camper registration fees. In addition, there is an annual renewal fee of several hundred dollars.

Over the years, the average investment required to develop and operate a quality campground has risen. There are relatively few shoestring or part-time operations today that are run with much success. Many enterprises start too small and never build up enough clientele to be successful.

Financing has been a persistent problem for the recreation industry, although lending institutions are becoming more supportive. Problems that concern lenders include the seasonal nature of many recreation and tourism businesses, the limited managerial ability of operators, and the limited equity involved in the mortgages. New owners must often put up personal collateral. Loans may be easier to obtain for those who are associated with a nationally known franchise.

Besides starting with a large enough investment, there are other keys to success in the campground business that are just as important. Location is closely identified with profitability. Accessibility to population centers, resort areas, and/or major highways seems to be important. Prior experience in the campground business is also important. The types of special or convenience services offered can have an effect. Hot showers and flush toilets are generally expected, although primitive camp sites may also be offered.

There are many drawbacks to entering the campground business. Private campgrounds have traditionally had to charge more than public campgrounds. In fact, government competition through subsidized low-cost camping has caused many operators to drop out of the campground business after years of marginal operation. Financing and insurance are often hard to get. Local, State, and Federal requirements regarding public health, sewage, water, safety, taxes, and liability have been difficult for many businesses to meet. The business is extremely demanding of time, especially during the season.

The manager must be able to do some of everything, from fixing a septic system to displaying merchandise attractively. Good hosting and management skills, and patience and friendliness with people are absolutely essential. One of the key competitive advantages that private campgrounds can offer over public campgrounds is a greater degree of personal attention from the campground owners and staff, and it is critical to a campground's success to maximize this advantage. To reduce the impact of low-occupancy days, many campgrounds offer seasonal or year-round rates.

Campgrounds often take on the look of a trailer park under this arrangement, but, on the other hand, regular customers often make a special effort to keep their places neat. Many recreation businesses have organized in order to promote their mutual interests and to have a greater voice in state and local government. There are campground associations in many countries.

Other Recreation Businesses

Vacation complexes, organization camps, guest ranches, and ski resorts are among the oldest elements of the recreation industry in forest areas. Many such enterprises have their base of operations on private lands but use public lands, especially national forest lands, for some activities. Fishing and swimming lakes and ponds, off-road vehicle trails, riding stables, and picnicking areas are other attractions.

There are shooting preserves and many leased hunting lands that take advantage of forest lands. Sporting clays are becoming very popular in some areas because they offer the sport and challenge of shooting without the limitation of seasons and without killing any wildlife. Sporting clays offer a variety of simulated game shoots as the shooter stalks through the forest and field, attempting to shoot clay pigeons that simulate a rabbit, duck, quail, or other game species.

The initial cost is in establishing trails through the woods and setting up the springloaded throwers. The sport can be as simple or elaborate as desired. The cost of building the trails could even be offset by selling firewood removed. For landowners who are contemplating a shooting preserve, the addition of a sporting clays activity gives diversity and extends their income opportunities. Some of these recreational activities might support a club activity on a seasonal basis. For example, acreage that is leased to a hunting club in the fall might be leased to a horseback riding club in the spring and summer.

Risk Recreation

Risk or adventure recreation differs from traditional outdoor recreation by posing elements of real or perceived physical danger to the participant. Possible income-producing risk recreation ventures related to forest lands might include the following:

Adventure travel	Backpacking
Hang gliding	Hot-air ballooning
Canoeing	Caving
Kayaking	Mountaineering
Hiking	Ice climbing
Orienteering	Rafting

- Mountain biking
- Ropes courses
- Rappelling
- Ski touring
- Skydiving
- Bicycle touring
- Mountain running
- Snowshoeing
- Rock climbing
- Winter camping
- Wilderness trekking

The income opportunities for risk recreation generally are either through fees for access to private land or through commercial operations. A variety of program elements might make up a recreation package. For example, a weekend introductory ski-touring package might include sales and rental, transportation, lodging, a pass to ski on groomed trails, meals, and classes. A package for more experienced participants might include transportation to and from a trailhead, winter camping, and a guided back-country ski tour on ungroomed trails.

In general, the profitability of recreational access ventures can vary greatly among divergent geographic, cultural, land use, and clientele situations. Information on patterns of demand should be used in assessing the feasibility of marketing recreational opportunities. For example, nature photographers require access to scenic views or wildlife populations.

Cross-country skiers require a more extensive land area than picnickers and may be willing to travel longer distances to participate. Commercial recreation ventures generally require sizeable acreage, large capital investments, and welltrained labor. Furthermore, the real costs of increased liability and management must be considered. People paying for recreation have a legal claim to safety in most cases, making a vendor much more liable for death or injury to recreationists than for trespassers. Some stables have been driven out of business by liability insurance costs.

Marketing

Advertising in well-known hunting magazines is very effective for hunting operations. These include Field and Stream, Outdoor Life, Ducks Unlimited, Wildfowl, Gun Dog, American Hunter, and Peterson Hunting. Ads generally run for a part of the year. Each ad should list services offered, address for a free brochure, and a telephone number. The brochure is very important, as is the treatment which someone inquiring on the phone receives.

Most fair-sized cities have annual shows for sports enthusiasts. Operators should rent space in at least two shows per year and pass out "free admission" coupons where appropriate. Trade shows help expand the marketing area and may be done in conjunction with a local chamber of commerce. Press releases and personal contacts with outdoor writers are inexpensive ways to get the word out to people about a recreation enterprise. Many outdoor writers welcome material for their columns. Most States have an outdoor writers association, and their mailing lists can usually be acquired.

Flyers, brochures, and posters can be distributed locally. Boy Scouts, Cub Scouts, retirement villages, churches and synagogues, and sporting goods stores are good starting points. Small ads in local newspapers are good for recreation operations. The ads can also include "free admission" coupons. Local television shows can provide good opportunities for marketing as well.

Infrastructural Needs

Achieving the appropriate quality of recreational experience requires the basics of clean, comfortable lodgings, good food, and a quality of naturalness. Structures should be designed to complement the landscape wherever possible.

Wildlife habitat improvements of an obviously artificial character such as nesting boxes made of plastic pipe, wire, and old tires should be avoided. Trails should be rustic, and signs should be tasteful and low profile.

Equipment needs vary according to the sophistication of the operation. For example, in the case of a fishing operation, the facility needs a small building for checking customers in and out, and, associated with that building, should be space to store and sell bait, lend stringers, clean fish, and store ice. The operation must be as clean, neat, and attractive as possible.

Labor needs will vary according to the type of enterprise being considered. For example, guides must be carefully selected and trained, since they are the individuals who spend the most time with customers. Retirees or college students often make good guides. When possible, entrepreneurs should consider employing family labor. Other ways to hold down labor costs are to swap help in an operation with friends or neighbors in exchange for hunting, fishing, or other recreational opportunities.

A recreation enterprise may require a significant investment in both facilities and new skills, including specialized management. A certain sensitivity to social processes and the social needs of groups of people is often also necessary. People who pay for recreational access are likely to be seeking highquality experiences and may expect special considerations.

The landowner who shares those expectations will be better able to anticipate particular needs and provide for them. In addition, marketing skills are exceedingly important in the success of recreation enterprises. Many cooperative extension or small business development centers offer courses in management.

Liability insurance rates vary widely for recreational enterprises. Sōme landowners are able to get amendments to comprehensive farm policies at reasonable rates. Prior to the establishment of any recreational enterprise, it would be essential to consult the local planning and zoning board as well as an insurance company and an attorney for details on these types of ventures.

Many countries have cooperative programs that offer landowners some form of economic inducement to allow recreational access. In these programs, the landowner agrees to make property accessible to recreationists in exchange for free technical services, wildlife plantings, signs for delineating property boundaries, and law enforcement patrol. For example, the Department of Wildlife and Parks in the State of Kansas encourages private landowners to enter their land into a public access program that allows recreational hunting. The agency posts the lands, assumes liability for recreational activities, and provides law enforcement.

Protection of property from illegal fishing or hunting is essential in providing the proper business environment for wildlife enterprises. Lack of control over property is usually the greatest limiting factor in preventing owners from developing wildlife opportunities on their properties. Strongly enforced, effective trespass laws are essential to the development of wildlife enterprises on wildlands. Most States need to increase the amount of fines and penalties for poaching and trespass.

Resource Conservation

For fishing and hunting operations, basic decisions must be made concerning the carrying capacity and sustainable yield of an area's land and water resources and the economic relevance of this yield to the success of the operation. Another factor to consider is the size of the home range of the animals. Species whose populations vary widely because of poor or good annual reproduction are more difficult to manage for wildlife recreational enterprises.

If a forest landowner is fortunate enough to host a population of a threatened or endangered plant or animal species, the survival of the species must take precedence over its value as an attraction. But if a buffer zone between the imperiled species' principal range and the conflicting human activities can be provided, it may be possible for the landowner to gain a special market niche by providing a chance of seeing a rare creature at a distance.

Managing Marine Wildlife Tourism

Wild fauna are particularly important ecotourism attractions. There ts a growing concern over the impacts of tourist interaction with marine wildlife and the disruption to natural processes. Despite many countries and agencies looking towards ecotourism as an answer to both economic and conservation objectives many remain unconvinced that such ventures are a panacea that both protects the environment and supports economic activity. Both Miossec's and Butler's widely reported models of tourism development conclude that tourism development eventually leads to a state of decline due to attraction degradation. Considerable debate exists therefore over whether eco-tourism can be sustainable and what management regimes/ strategies can be employed to minimise the negative impacts which are associated with anthropogenic influences on natural ecosystems.

Management Techniques

The techniques which have traditionally been utilised to

manage visitor use of parks and protected natural areas can be divided into three main categories.

First, physical controls in the form of barriers, paths, boardwalks, and the location of facilities are used to influence visitor behaviour. Visitor impacts are thereby reduced by physically separating them from the natural environment or by influencing the spatial distribution of use in order to protect sensitive areas.

Second, direct controls in the form of rules, regulations, permits and charges are often imposed and enforced in order to prohibit or restrict human behaviour which may be detrimental to the natural environment. For example, by banning certain activities, setting speed limits, requiring permits, closing areas and enforcing these controls with fines, forced removal from an area, banning future entry, arrests and prosecutions.

Third, indirect mechanisms which seek to reduce inappropriate behaviour on a voluntary basis through education are increasingly utilised. These kinds of environmental education programs are termed 'interpretation' and were first widely advocated by Tilden. The assumption implicit in interpretive programs is that visitors are motivated to minimise their impact on the natural enviromnent.

Interpretive-based Management Strategies

Numerous examples of interpretation of the natural environment show that they not only help to protect the environment but that they also increase visitor enjoyment. Interpretation is therefore seen as a 'win-win' situation for park managers and park visitors. Parks, protected natural areas and private sector, nature-based tourism operations have primarily managed tourist use of the natural environment on the basis of the first two management categories. However, the role of interpretation as an effective management strategy is seen as being increasingly important.

Environmental education is no longer a frill or a luxury. It is an essential management fimction for every park, recreation area, and refuge to undertake.

The continuing challenge is to provide opportunities for wildlife oriented recreation that preserve ecosystem integrity. Each cautious experiment helps to better define the limits of what is possible. Much of recreational demand will have to be satisfied through environmental education and interpretation. Traditionally, interpretive programs have been carried out by governmental resource management agencies such as park and reserves departments, forestry and land management bureaus. However, more recently private operators and tourist resorts have recognised the importance of interpretive techniques in responding to the needs of nature oriented tourists and protecting the attractions they wish to visit.

Despite this expanding support for interpretation as a management technique there is little empirical research which assesses the effectiveness of such strategies. There is a need to conduct studies of the use of various types of educational programs in order to analyse successful and unsuccessful efforts and subsequently to eshblish general guidelines which can assist management in designing and implementing such programs.

General interpretive model

A basis for the design and testing of interpretive programs is proposed by Forestell and Kaufman. As a result of a review of cognitive pyschological theory and the study of whale watchers in Hawaii they conclude that an effective interpretation program for marine wildlife has three main stages.

Figure 1 illustrates these stages. Firstly, 'dynamic disequilibrium' should be created or promoted. This simply stated, involves creating a perceived need for information and thereby a motivation to learn. The intention of this stage of the model is to create questions in the mind of the tourist rather than answer them. The authors argue that this strategy should be adopted prior to tourist's contact with the wildlife.

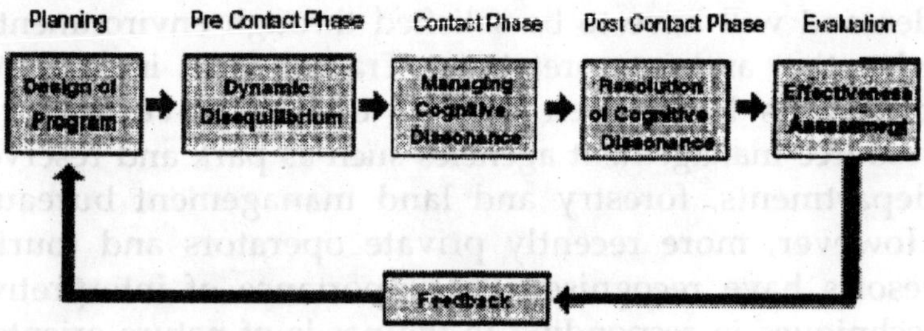

Figure 1. A general interpretive model

During the tourists contact with the animals the 'cognitive dissonance' created during the pre-contact phase needs to be managed. That is, the needed information should be provided in an informed and interesting manner and should be relevant to what the tourist is observing and experiencing. Finally, the 'resolution of cognitive dissonance' should be undertaken and action strategies should be outlined. This involves the broadening' of the experience and new information into a consideration of wider marine environmental issues and encouraging the tourists to internalise their knowledge and incorporate the new information into changed behaviour.

A subsequent phase needs to be added to the model; 'evaluation' of the effectiveness of the program should be undertaken and the findings 'fed back' into program planning. The general features outlined by Forestell and Kaufman can form the basic structure from which a situation specific interpretation program is developed. Subsequent testing and analysis of the effectiveness of interpretive programs in differing situations could establish guidelines which will be of considerable assistance in the planning and management of wildlife and nature-based tourism.

Ecotourism has been hailed as an acceptable and desirable form of use of the marine environment. however, many are justifiably cynical about the 'dressing up' of exploitive use of the natural environment under a new and more acceptable name. Despite these concerns, and the acknowledgement of the rapidly increasing demand for interaction with wildlife in natural settings, there have been few investigations into the effectiveness of varying management regimes. There is therefore, a need to establish the most successful management techniques which protect marine fauna and allow for tourist interaction.

5

Coastal Tourism Management

Coastal tourism and recreation are important parts of the largest and most rapidly growing activity in international tourism. Tourism and recreation-related development is one of the major factors shaping development patterns in the coastal zones of many countries. Coastal tourism provides significant economic benefits.

The term 'coastal tourism and recreation' embraces the full range of tourism, leisure, and recreationally oriented activities that take place in the coastal zone and the offshore coastal waters. These include coastal tourism development (hotels, resorts, restaurants, food industry, vacation homes, second homes, etc.), and the infrastructure supporting coastal development (retail businesses, marinas, fishing tackle stores, dive shops, fishing piers, recreational boating harbors, beaches, recreational fishing facilities, and the like).

Of all the activities that take place in coastal zones and the near-shore coastal ocean, none is increasing in both volume and diversity more than coastal tourism and recreation. Both the dynamic nature of this sector and its magnitude demand that ~~it~~ be actively taken into account in government plans, policies, and programs related to the coasts and ocean. Indeed, virtually all coastal and ocean issue areas affect coastal tourism and recreation either directly or indirectly. Clean water, healthy coastal habitats, and a safe, secure, and enjoyable environment are clearly fundamental to successful coastal tourism. Similarly, bountiful living marine resources (fish, shellfish, wetlands, coral reefs, etc.) are of critical importance to most recreational experiences. Security from risks associated with natural coastal hazards such as storms, hurricanes, tsunamis, and the like is a requisite for coastal tourism to be sustainable over the long term.

The coasts and coastal waters are of great value to the nativepeople both for their personal enjoyment and for the economic benefits these areas generate for coastal communities, coastal states, and for the nation as a whole benefits that can be sustainable indefinitely with proper foresight and enlightened public policies. But, these benefits cannot be taken for granted. Coastal habitats and the resources they support must be protected and, where necessary, restored.

The quality of coastal waters must be maintained at a sufficiently high level to provide a healthy and aesthetically pleasing environment for water-based recreation. Similarly, swimming beaches must be maintained at an attractive and functional level even in the presence of accelerating sea-level rise and associated erosion, and possible increases in the frequency of coastal storms. The maintenance of safe conditions for recreational boating and underwater recreation (e.g., adequately marked waterways, timely weather information, rescue services, hyperbaric chambers, etc.) is also of great importance.

The precise magnitude of tourism in coastal and marine areas is not clear, since no separate statistics are kept for foreign or domestic tourists to these areas. Figures on foreign tourism receipts are generally based on surveys of departing travelers, generating data which are "imperfect and cannot be compared over time with precision. Data on tourism in coastal areas cannot easily be disaggregated from national-level statistics, but impressionistic evidence as well as a number of recent works on the subject suggest continued growth of tourism in coastal and marine areas in the United States and worldwide. Detailed information on the economic impact of domestic tourism has been difficult to find, but growth in all forms of recreation in coastal areas in which both foreign and domestic tourists partake is readily apparent. Such activities include beach going, recreational boating, cruises, marine mammal watching, recreational fishing, underwater recreation, bird watching, nature appreciation, and the like.

Impact of Tourism on Coastal Areas

Coastal and marine resources throughout the world have suffered major impacts by human actions since early colonial days. A synthesis of major impacts conveys a picture in which virtually every country suffers from sewage pollution of coastal waters, most suffer some contamination from oil spills and production leakages, a majority of countries report coastal pollution from mining and industrial activity, and most of the low income countris report solid waste contamination of coastal areas. In addition, many countries report inadequate monitoring and assessment systems to understand what is really happening in the first place.

Tourism has direct and indirect impacts on the surrounding envirionment. If tourism facilities and activities result in a high degree of environmental impact, it is likely that tourism will be reduced. These problems can compound themselves if the reduction in tourists causes loss in income which results in curtailment of essential services (e.g., operation and oversight of sewage treatment plants) which further alienates tourists.

Available evidence confirms that the environmental effects of tourism activities in coastal areas occur within national boundaries. The major tourism effects in coastal areas are:

— Displacement of Traditional Uses and Users

— Physical Changes and Habitat Damage

— Solid Waste Disposal

— Toxic Chemicals and Nutrification from Surface Runoff

— Groundwater Depletion and Contamination

— Change in Sediment Loads

— Visual Impacts

Tourism Facilities in Coastal Zones

There are six categories of tourism facility. These categories are designed to capture the bulk of tourism activity, but they are not meant to be totally comprehensive or exclusive. That is, for example, a tourism complex could include large and small hotels, restaurants and beach recreational facilities. These categories refer to the activities of tourists, services provided to tourists, and the necessary infrastructure to support those services.

— Tourism Complexes and Large Resorts

— Marine Recreational Facilities

— Small Hotels and Resorts

— Entertainment Facilities

— Shoreside Recreational Facilities

— Parks and Protected Areas

The "coastal zone" is not a homogeneous, easily demarcated area. It includes a variety of geological and environmental systems which are impacted and react differently to stress caused by coastal tourism activities. There are three general areas of impact: 1) mainland, 2) coast, and 3) ocean; and three directions to look for environmental effects: 1) inland, 2) along the coast, and 3) seaward.

Environmental degradation effects can be reduced by best management practices from a number of disciplines outside the coastal environment and tourism planning sector. Best management practices for tourism can be supported by broad involvement and information sharing among several sectors, such as agriculture, forestry, hydrology, public works, and environmental health.

Stimulating best management practices for coastal tourism means shaping the tools for linking potential impacts with mitigation information. As an example, the matrix shows few references which deal with impacts on groundwater resources or sediment loading. But clearly there are hundreds of works on hydrology, landscape engineering and architecture which could be mustered to address these problems, if broad-ranging information sharing for environmental impact reduction and mitigation is given a priority.

Management Requirements

This section lists requirements for management practices which should be addressed by elements of the tourism industry. Major categories include:

— development of tourism facilities, especially resorts, hotels and other major construction activities;

— site and building design

— energy management

— water supply

— waste prevention
— facility maintenance and operations
— cultural effects and displacement of traditional activities.

Coastal Tourism Planning

A perusal of the literature on tourism suggests that it is easy to make generalizations: on the positive side, to extol its huge economic development potential; on the negative side, to decry impacts on the environment, overuse of resources and energy, ignorance of local culture, and absence of local benefits. For analytical purposes, it is best, however, to consider tourism in neutral terms as an agent of development and change which may have both positive and negative effects.

Tourism, like other industries, is an agent of development and change and must be recognized as such. It is consumptive like any other industry and the level of consumption is determined by the scale and style of tourism development. At low levels and with careful design, tourism may be able to operate at a sustainable level. However, controlling the level and style of development over the long term presents challenges which, to this point, have not been successfully met. Because of its potentially high impact, tourism should be considered in the same manner as any other industry and should be subjected to the same environmental and social impact assessment processes during the planning stages.

Tourism has often been ignored by public sector agencies. Where it has been considered as a specific development feature, it has often been viewed as a "soft" option, which can be pursued relatively easily and which does not require much in terms of specific planning or resources. While this view has changed somewhat in recent years as the magnitude and importance of tourism has begun to be appreciated, ignorance about tourism and many of the processes associated with it is still widespread.

The lack of attention by public agencies to tourism is especially problematic in the case of marine and coastal tourism. In most countries, there usually is no coordination between programs that promote and market tourism and those that manage coastal and marine areas. Integrated coastal management often tends to be done within environmental or planning agencies. On the other hand, agencies dealing with the promotion of tourism are not involved with the evaluation of its effects or with advance planning and management of the adverse impacts of tourism through avoidance, mitigation, and compensation strategies. Hence, one of the greatest challenges facing coastal managers is how to integrate tourism development within the ambit of integrated coastal management, and thus increase the likelihood of long-term sustainability.

In the management of tourism development planning and construction, there is a strong incentive to address negative pollution effects directly. It is the task of public sector managers and monitors to ensure that pollution prevention or mitigation activities do not merely displace pollution to other less visible sites or less powerful communities. For physical processes and biological systems, project design reviews need to adhere to limits on acceptable change and the introduction of exotic species.

Placing limits on acceptable change is a tourism management practice which is being developed to replace the less realistic "carrying capacity" concept. Limits on acceptable change attempt to assess stress in both the natural and the social and economic environment, to define the maximum degree of change which is tolerable.

The concept is realistic in suggesting the "political" costs of limiting further development which could be seen to reduce employment growth and to deprive the affected region of modern infrastructure and other benefits.

A Coastal Zone Management Program has to develop a large number of best management practices which can be adapted for a variety of tourism-related facilities, especially for the smaller national or regional programs working with tourism development. The major practices should be included are:

— Studies of baseline environmental conditions for all major projects

— Standardized monitoring requirements for physical, environmental and water quality conditions;

— A series of detailed construction practice principles for the marine area to mitigate construction impacts, including:

  — Clean materials and equipment;

  — Repair equipment away from the beach;

  — Use suction dredges;

  — Use turbidity barriers to protect reefs;

  — Set standards for suspending work based on turbidity over reefs;

  — Clearly buoy reefs, seagrass, and other sensitive areas for construction periods;

  — Carefully place anchors and semi-permanent moorings;

  — Minimize vehicle movement to reduce compacting of beach sand and use care in storing materials;

  — Special steps to protect turtles, including avoiding construction during nesting season, avoiding lights on the beach at night, relocating fresh nests, and so on.

In the extensively used and abused coastal areas which are premium sites for tourism facilities, the land is more damaged than is commonly appreciated by visitors and developers. Furthermore, a wide variety of stresses, including density of settlement, air quality concerns, and marine pollutants, are damaging the ability of natural systems to recover from trauma caused by natural or manmade disasters. Site design considerations must stem from a respect for the landscape and an effort to understand the relationships among soil, water, plant communities and associations, and habitats.

A sustainable approach to site planning and building design starts with traditional practices of inventorying the principal factors of the site, and then goes on to determine the relationships among the factors of the site and how these factors will adapt to change and to the physical structures to be added to the site. The design should include an environmental model which describes the essential functions and interrelationships of the site factors.

Coastal Management and Planning Programmes

The United States has the oldest national coastal management and planning program in the world, initiated under the Coastal Zone Management Act of 1972. The program, administered by NOAA's Office of Ocean and Coastal Resource Management, now includes coastal management programs in 31 U.S. states and territories, covering 97.2 percent of the U.S. shoreline. The program uses incentives (in the form of grants to the states and the "federal consistency" provision) to assist states in the preparation and implementation of coastal management plans. These state efforts have been multifaceted and have addressed, through a variety of means, all uses of coastal areas.

Three management practices under the Coastal Zone Management (CZM) program are especially important for ensuring sustainable tourism development:

(1) provisions for the management of coastal development;

(2) provisions to improve public access to the shoreline; and

(3) provisions to protect coastal environments.

The CZM programs should have elements which, in effect, help manage coastal development. Two of these are especially relevant to tourism development:

(1) encouragement of water-dependent uses in the coastal zone and

(2) the appropriate siting of new facilities in the coastal zone.

CZM programs should actively encourage and facilitate the use of land adjacent to the shoreline for those purposes which require such a location. This policy helps ensure that proposals for tourism and marine recreation projects receive appropriate consideration in the government review process. It should also helps ensure that meritorious coastal tourism developments are not crowded out of the coastal zone by uses that do not require a shoreside location.

Construction of new facilities in the coastal zone must meet the setback requirements of state CZM programs. While states differ in their requirements, the trend is to relate setback lines to annual erosion rates and, thus, to require the greatest setbacks from the high tidemark in those areas having the largest erosion rates. Facilities siting policies also help ensure that new tourism construction is not located in hazardous areas from the standpoint of coastal storm damage and flooding.

A strong emphasis in many coastal zone management programs relate to the importance of ensuring adequate public access to the shorelines for recreational pursuits. All most all such programs are actively pursuing this goal. For example, Since 1980, for example, the California Coastal Program has acquired over 2,300 public access ways along the coast while the San Francisco Bay Conservation and Development Commission has increased public access around the perimeter of San Francisco Bay from 4 miles in 1977 to more than 96 miles in 1990. Under the CZM program, states and localities use grant funding and regulatory tools to secure improved public access for recreational purposes. The existence of healthy coastal habitats is important to coastal recreation and tourism. CZM programs represent one of the important management avenues in obtaining this protection. Within specified coastal zone boundaries, states and/or their local governments regulate activities which could adversely impact these habitats. Other coastal area protection programmes also serve to protect coastal habitats.

Ecological Approach to Tourism Coastal Management

Ecotourism or nature tourism is: "Tourism that involves traveling to relatively undisturbed or uncontaminated natural areas with the specific object of studying, admiring, and enjoying the scenery and its wild plants and animals, as well as any existing cultural areas." While still relatively small, ecotourism is one of the fastest growing segments of the tourism industry and presents special management challenges. Internationally, ecotourism is growing at a moderate rate with the financial impacts greatest in rural areas near important ecotourism activities. In 1988, international ecotourists numbered 236 million worldwide, with an estimated economic impact of $233 billion.

Ecotourism in association with marine and estuarine protected areas. However, for ecotourism activities to be sustainable, they must be managed properly and with special care. Unless properly managed, the impacts of ecotourism may be worse than those of tourism to clearly defined and confined resorts. In the United States, for example, concerns have been raised about the impacts of ecotourism on marine mammals, which are protected under the Marine Mammal Protection Act.

Commercial cruises to observe and "feed wild dolphins" operating in such areas as Texas, South Carolina, and Florida, were found to harm dolphins by making them reliant on accepting food from humans and decreasing their ability to survive in the wild. Threats to the marine mammal populations and to humans in these situations include:

(1) substantially altering the natural behavior of marine mammals, including foraging for food and migration,

(2) the loss of wariness by humans, which places the animals at increased risk of injury or death from interaction with vessels,

(3) animals receiving inappropriate or contaminated food, and

(4) increased injuries to humans as the habituated animals become predictably more aggressive when they lose their wariness of humans and compete for handouts.

Tools and Techniques

Although coastal tourism constitutes a strong force (both positive and negative) in shaping coastal communities and local, regional, and national economies, coastal tourism is generally not seen as a specific sector requiring policy, planning, and management attention and resources. This is due, in part, to the fact that data and information tend not be gathered and aggregated under this heading. Hence, the magnitude and importance of leisure and recreationally motivated development in the coastal zone tends to be understated, understudied, and under-managed.

However, certain aspects of this situation may be changing. Since the Earth Summit in Rio de Janeiro in 1992, a number of new initiatives for sustainable tourism practices have appeared. For example, in 1993, a new periodical entitled Journal of Sustainable Tourism appeared, focusing on applying the principles of sustainable development to the tourism field.

In 1997, on the occasion of the five-year review of the implementation of Earth Summit agreements, three organizations: The World Travel and Tourism Council, the World Tourism Organization, and the Earth Council; jointly published *Agenda 21 for the Travel and Tourism Industry: Towards Environmentally Sustainable Development*. This report presents a summary of Agenda 21 (one of the main outputs of the Earth Summit), and the role that travel and tourism can play in achieving the goals of Agenda 21. It also outlines a program of action.

Planning for sustainable tourism development is one of the priority areas of the program, which calls for complementarity between tourism and coastal development by adopting suitable policies such as the Global Blue Flag Program. The Blue Flag Program is a European campaign started in the 1980s which encourages local authorities to provide clean and safe beaches for local populations and international tourists. Blue Flag awards go to beaches that achieve certain standards in water quality, beach management and safety, and environmental information and education. A guide for tourism managers has also been developed by the World Tourism Organization on the formulation and use of indicators of sustainable tourism. Indicators signal unacceptable levels of impacts or stress, and these can in turn lead to the development of standards to govern tourism activities. Core indicators developed by the WTO include use intensity, species counts, pollution levels and accident rates. New tools are also being developed in connection with coastal tourism and natural disasters, such as hurricanes.

Integrated Coastal Area Tourism Management

Integrated Coastal Area Management (ICAM) practices, especially as employed in programs such as the British Virgin Islands Town and Country Planning permit process (Louis Potter, Chief Physical Planner, personal communication), and the United States National Estuaries Program, provide opportunities for early intervention and collaborative review of tourism site planning. By publishing public standards and goals in advance of the submission of plans by private developers, these programs are able to provide guidance before major investments are made in site development. These standards also provide objective measures which can be used by community and environmental NGOs to question specific elements of development proposals. These planning programs differ from the coastal engineering and restoration objectives of other coastal zone management programs, such as the program of the Barbados Coastal Zone Management Unit, or the Northwest Coastal Zone Program in St. Lucia.

Energy Management

Many tourism facilities suffer from inappropriate energy use models transferred without appropriate modification from temperate areas. In addition, rapid social and economic change has created a need to design simultaneously for energy efficiency and for difficult problems of high land costs, noise, and physical security. Ecotourism resorts have been leaders in pushing for the use of renewable energy resources. For the proposed 150-unit Concordia Estates eco-condo development on the island of St. John in the US Virgin Islands, for example, ecotourism promoter Stanley Selengut has applied for permits to install seven 100-foot towers to assess the feasibility of wind energy systems to power the resort.

There are abundant sources of guidance for both design considerations for minimizing unnecessary energy use and for better control of energy intensive operating practices. Some of the measures most commonly recommended and adopted include:

- signage and notes to remind tourists to participate in energy conservation by turning out lights, maintaining moderate air-conditioning operation, and moderate use of hot water;
- solar water heaters;
- designs for open-air public spaces in hotels and resorts;
- motion detectors for room lighting;
- re-engineering of kitchen areas;
- replacement of appliances (e.g., refrigerators) in rooms with more modern, more energy efficient versions;
- reduced-wattage, low-energy, or solar-powered (e.g., for pathway lights) lighting systems.

Water Pollution Management

The Office of Wetlands, Oceans and Watersheds of the United States Environmental Protection Agency (USEPA) published Guidance Specifying Management Measures for Sources of Nonpoint Pollution in Coastal Waters in 1993, which provides a number of important resources for management practices for coastal tourism. As employed by the USEPA, there are five areas of guidance, including agriculture, forestry, urban areas, marinas and recreational boating, and hydromodification. All of these guidance areas except forestry have elements which need to be adapted and applied to tourism activities.

The agricultural management guidance identifies measures to reduce and mitigate sediment runoff, nutrients and pesticides. Sediment is a major contaminant from tourism construction, which needs to be controlled by improved design for slowing runoff and by practices which control runoff across vulnerable construction sites. Nutrient and pesticide management are important for landscaping, and in the design and operation of septic sewage systems. Irrigation activities on hotel and resort properties can be major contributors to depletion of groundwater resources and intrusion of saltwater.

Improved Landscaping Practices

The groundskeeper training programs provide both a high standard of training in the use of indigenous plants for resort landscaping, and especially in proper use of chemicals and water to minimize impacts. A community-focussed "horticulture" newsletter was a popular by-product of this program. It should be noted that these practices are in contrast to other all-inclusive resorts which conduct landscaping with a standardized catalogue of exotic plants which are planted to reflect the resort's signature "look," whether that is appropriate to local environment conditions or resources.

The management guidance for urban areas includes measures to control sediment, nutrients, biological oxygen demand, heavy metals and hydrocarbons and biological contamination. These latter elements suggest a series of design and construction activities which will help avoid direct discharges from roadways and parking lots into adjacent rivers and coastal waters. Sewage treatment strategies and the placement of outfalls are important tourism considerations.

Recreational boating management measures which will protect near coastal water quality include:

— adequate marina flushing design;

— rigorous water quality and habitat assessments;

— runoff control from the marina, including injections from boat cleaning areas;

— fuel station design and operations;

— sewage and solid waste control;

— disposal of fish wastes; and

— boat operation.

Modification of shorelines, channels and the land under the sea from bulldozing, bulkheading, filling and dredging can have direct physical effects on land and habitat, and water quality effects may have more extensive consequences (following the plume from the site of the disturbance) for wildlife, reefs, and bottom-dwelling communities.

Waste Management

Best management practices for solid waste generated within the tourism industry require design of elements within tourism facilities which make it clear how tourists can properly dispose of waste, and periodic waste audits by tourism facility managers to highlight gaps in current waste management flows.

Solid waste management issues have received considerable attention in recent years, with best management practices developed for both land-based pollution and ship-generated waste. There are currently two GEF projects and two World Bank-funded projects in the Caribbean dealing with solid waste management issues, and the Meeting of Environmental Technical Experts follow-up to the Summit of the Americas dealt with a number of solid waste management issues relevant to tourism.

In addition to the simple expedient of making tourist waste management facilities visible and accessible, it is necessary to devote resources to the maintenance of these systems and in the training and orientation of tourism facilities staff in the waste management strategy. These activities require a considerable investment in public awareness and public education programs, including inculcating in facility operators that they are "hosts" with a responsibility to both maintain their home, and to stimulate responsible behavior by visitors.

Liquid waste management practices need to be better coordinated with water supply concerns and national strategies for groundwater recharge and maintenance of groundwater quality. Because of the need to reduce the drawdown of freshwater resources, many more tourism facilities in the coastal area need to consider alternatives for treatment and re-injection of gray water systems.

Management of Clean Water and Healthy Ecosystems

Clean water and healthy coastal ecosystems are essential to the maintenance of coastal tourism and recreation. Foreign tourists and the recreating domestic public stop going to areas where the waters are polluted, beaches are closed, or fish are tainted. For example, it is reported that the State of New Jersey lost $800 million in tourism revenues following reports that medical wastes had washed up on some of its beaches.

According to EPA estimates, coastal and marine waters support 28.3 million jobs, generate $54 billion in goods and services, contribute $30 billion to the U.S. economy through recreational fishing, and provide a destination for 180 million Americans to recreate each year. In the past 25 years, there have been extensive efforts made by federal agencies, especially EPA and NOAA, in association with the coastal states, to improve coastal water quality. Under programs authorized by the Clean Water Act of 1972 and administered by EPA, significant improvements in water quality have been realized. Point sources have been largely controlled under the National Pollution Discharge Elimination System (NPDES). Significant challenges remain regarding the control of non-point sources of water pollution, especially in coastal areas abutting agricultural lands.

Protection of the marine environment is one of the critical services provided by coast guard. This includes prevention of environmentally threatening marine accidents and responses aimed at minimizing adverse effects should accidents occur., This also includes protection of living marine resources and marine sanctuaries.

Facility Maintenance and Operations

Facility maintenance and operations need to be considered from the beginning of the design process. For major facilities the maintenance and operations plan should be part of the approval process for the facility. Maintenance and operations are not, however, constrained only to hotels and resorts. In fact, because maintenance and operations management practices affect almost all levels of overnight visitor facilities, plus most of the coastal recreational and entertainment facilities, they are especially significant in limiting negative environmental effects.

In addition, tourism-focused maintenance and operations activities have a large carryover and demonstration effect on practices employed by people in other sectors. For example, if pesticide applicators working in the tourism sector employ safe practices, these are likely to be employed in treating private homes.

Sustainable design features for the maintenance and operation of tourism facilities include the specification of durable or recyclable materials, designs for low energy consumption, user-friendly operation, properly trained staff and oversight by experienced management. Maintenance implications for commonly used construction materials are well known to facility designers in temperate areas.

Among the management features of a maintenance and operations system are:

— An inventory of all elements to maintain.

— Locally adapted maintenance standards, reflecting especially the extra efforts required by the warmth and high moisture which characterizes coastal environments.

— Work schedules accounting for local work practices and holiday and vacation practices.

— Work practices, including training and controls for third party contractors often used for many maintenance functions. In areas where contractors provide a large portion of the total services with important environmental effects, such as lawn services or septic system maintenance, national authorities need to consider direct control of the performance of such services, rather than relying on managers of resorts or tourist facilities to police these environmental impacts.

— Logistical services including extra storage requirements for maintenance and replacement of items with long stocking times. The logistic plan should also include a process for periodically reviewing available suppliers to determine the most environmentally benign supplies.

— Realistic long- and short-term budgets. Many development proposals budget only for the early periods of the project, before maintenance and replacements costs for major features of the development begin.

Management of Coastal Recreation Activities

The last decade has seen a great increase in the nature and magnitude of coastal recreation activities, which as has been shown, generate billions of dollars in economic activity. Recreational uses of a consumptive nature include hunting, fishing, shellfishing, shell collection, and the like, while non-consumptive uses include swimming, surfing, sun-bathing, boating, wind-surfing, jet skiing, bird watching, snorkeling, diving, glass-bottom boating, and many more. As coastal recreation activities have proliferated, the need for active management has increased as well.

At least three sets of concerns related to the management of coastal recreation activities must be dealt with, namely, environmental/resource concerns, amenity concerns, and safety concerns. Environmental/resource constraints include the maintenance of good water quality, and habitats and living resources which are free of health hazards, and which have good air quality, healthy coral reefs, healthy shellfish areas, etc.

Amenity concerns include adequate controls on congestion, noise, landscape degradation, and the like. Safety concerns include adequate lifeguard systems, first aid facilities, telephones, codes of conduct for beach users, and notice systems for beach and water hazards (such as jellyfish, underwater obstructions, etc.) and for weather-related risks (such as high waves, undertows, dangerous currents, etc.).

In most cases, the responsibility for meeting these concerns is divided between the beach "owner" (often a local government or state government, but sometimes federal or private), resort and/or recreation facility operators, and state environmental or health departments. In general, nationwide standards for recreational beach operation do not exist, even with respect to beach closings. This would appear to be an area where additional attention at the national level is needed.

A promising start in this area is a new program recently launched by the EPA and designated the Beaches Environmental Assessment, Closure, and Health (BEACH) Program. This program is designed to encourage government agencies at all levels to strengthen beach water quality standards and testing methods using predictive water pollution models, to better inform the public about beach water quality conditions, and to make information about the risks associated with swimming in contaminated beach water available to the public.

Cultural Resources and Relocation of Traditional Activities

Cultural resources are reflections of past social, economic, historical and environmental conditions and events. Tourism activities in areas containing cultural resources or traditional activities should be encouraged to pursue appropriate procedures from initial planning through operations to ensure that these nonrenewable, environmentally sensitive resources are protected, conserved and interpreted for visitors and future generations.

Among the specific practices which need to be applied to the management of tourism areas with cultural resources or populations employing traditional practices are the following:

— Proposed development sites should be surveyed for cultural resources and traditional uses, and the significance and integrity of these should be documented prior to the consideration or approval of any tourism development proposal. This is the kind of activity which can be performed by properly trained and oriented volunteers, with the results archived as part of the profile of existing features which should be available in advance to any developers.

— Site and facility designs should include features which preserve and promote significant cultural features.

— Architectural style, landscape design and constructions materials should reflect local cultural elements.

— Cultural resource maintenance should be sustainable within the business plan of the proposed development.

— The operating plan of the proposed facility should include interpretation of cultural resources and opportunities to accommodate traditional practices.

Management of Coastal Hazards

In siting coastal resorts and other facilities, there is understandably a predilection for locating in beautiful but high-risk zones that are as close as physically possible to the edge of the sea, or otherwise take advantage of scenic views and proximity to beaches and ocean recreation. Of course, it is precisely these areas that are most vulnerable to both long-term and episodic coastal hazards: such as erosion, storms, and floods.

One of the few benefits of the high rate of natural hazards encountered in the coastal zones of those sub-regions most dependent on tourism is that periodic disasters provide an opportunity to correct conditions which have imposed unnecessary or unwise stresses on the local environment. Coastal areas are especially subject to severe damages from hurricanes, coastal and inland flooding, earthquakes and tsunamis. Global climate change is predicted to lead to sea level rise and possibly an increase in the frequency of severe ocean storms and hurricanes. This will increase the risks to tourism facilities, and the risk of environmental damages from such disasters.

In order to take advantage of these "opportunities," states must identify in advance those conditions or mitigation activities which should be implemented subsequent to a major disaster. For example, in a coastal resort area without adequate sewerage services, in the aftermath of a major hurricane the state could take advantage of the hurricane destruction to:

— limit reconstruction through a variety or regulatory and economic measures in order to reduce high densities on the coast;

— increase set-backs from the surf and dune line to reduce damages in subsequent storms and other disasters; and

— build new sewerage and other utility systems to more safely serve the new target population and tourist services

Discussions of rebuilding and hazard mitigation strategies to be employed in subsequent disasters can be conducted both in the context of coastal area planning activities, and also in special planning exercises organized with tourism investors and local communities in areas which have suffered most in the past, or which are predicted to suffer most in new disasters.

While government cannot be expected to protect individuals from their own recklessness, it does have a responsibility to provide the information necessary to permit informed decisions to be made with regard to the kinds and degrees of risk associated with living in various parts of the coastal zone. Furthermore, coastal areas that are clearly hazardous as building sites should be reserved for other uses. Government also has the responsibility to provide adequate warnings of impending storms or other hazardous conditions, and to develop plans for coping with such emergencies. Several government programs exist to meet these needs as discussed below.

In USA, at the federal level, FEMA's National Flood Insurance Program (NFIP) and the Coastal Zone Management Program exist, in part, to address these problems. The NFIP offers flood insurance to coastal landowners in communities that have met government standards for building in coastal areas. FEMA is also responsible for supporting and facilitating the work of state emergency preparedness offices in the preparation of coastal evacuation plans and plans to deal with disasters such as hurricanes both during the event and during the clean-up and reconstruction phases. NOAA's National Weather Service devotes considerable resources to the job of providing timely "state-of-the-art" forecasts and predictions of hurricanes and other coastal storms.

Through the federal CZM program, coastal states build in their own regulatory approaches such as construction setback lines, storm-resistant building codes, acquisition programs for hazardous areas, and the like.

Recognizing the connections that should exist between the planning and management efforts under CZM, and cognizant of the lessons being learned during storm events by the emergency management programs, NOAA and FEMA are initiating a series of workshops to strengthen the coordination between these programs.

Advanced planning and follow-up are required to maintain a safe and secure environment for visitors. Tourists take their safety for granted when they go to the beach or visit a coastal resort or even rent a sailboat for the day. Yet the coast is inherently a place with real risks, even under good weather conditions. Swimmers can drown and boats can collide or go aground, poisonous jellyfish can sting. And, of course, episodic large storms and hurricanes can have devastating consequences in coastal areas heavily populated with visitors.

Increasing numbers of people find themselves on the waterways in connection with recreational boating, fishing, traveling to and from coral reefs for snorkeling and diving, and so on. Maintaining an adequate level of safety and accident prevention requires properly marked channels, rescue services, oversight of boating safety requirements and monitoring and enforcement of boating operations, including so-called "thrill craft." While some of these duties can be performed by local and state authorities, the maintenance of safe and well-marked waterways and maritime safety in general has traditionally been a federal government responsibility. In any event, the federal government is in the best position to ensure than an adequately comprehensive safety program is in place in coastal areas.

Selecting Best Management Practices

This section provides guidance for private and public planners, managers, and policy makers for the adoption of best management practices by tourism facilities and support services. Each country with a major stake in tourism needs to define specific income and tourist goals for its development strategy. Studies of tourism cycles show a variety of tourism densities which tend to be reflected in tourism activitie. The most significant point of these studies is that there seems to be an inverse relationship between density of tourist activities and retained earnings per tourist.

A starting point for tourism planning is the array of broader environmental assessment and planning processes which have been developed, including environmental profiles, national environmental action plans or environmental strategies, and the recent move toward state-of-the-environment. Planning to mitigate the negative effects, and promote the positive effects of tourism, needs to be integrated into these larger frameworks wherever possible.

Public debate of tourism goals has several advantages to tourism development managers in both the private and public sector:

— It sets expectations for acceptable types and intensity of development;

— It helps to identify trade-offs between impact and potential benefits;

— It provides a negotiating mandate and framework for the permitting process;

— It emphasizes the need to protect environmental values throughout the nation to maintain an attractive tourism package;

— It can highlight areas which require remediation or restoration to avoid losing tourists.

Goal Setting

For countries which have the option to evaluate several styles of tourism, it is prudent to explore lower density, lower impact forms of tourism before opting for mass tourism approaches. Low density tourism options allow greater flexibility in moving local residents into management and ownership positions. Also, lower density forms of tourism provide opportunities to retain a higher proportion of local tourist expenditures, whereas mass tourism options almost always require the importation of more resources and services, including finances, management, and supplies.

Another reason for supporting more integrated public planning for tourism is that both the process and the plan it produces give developers and government program managers much clearer guidance for the kinds of mitigating steps or trade-offs that the local community is likely to endorse for a given type of development. In some communities, for example, providing jobs with strong supports for training and movement into management positions is the most important issue whereas other communities may be much more likely to respond positively to environmental restoration activities.

Remediation Planning

Public tourism planning programs also serve to identify critical needs for remediation planning, which can also be developed as a part of goal setting. There are many areas which are in danger of environmental collapse without corrective action by tourism-related businesses. For example, the fragile peat wetlands of Negril require major investments to recover from loss of water resources and pollution of aquifers and degraded coastal and estuarine areas. Similarly, Rodney Bay and the Pigeon Island causeway in St. Lucia require major changes in physical design and infrastructure to recover from early design and construction decisions. Problems like these can be developed within the framework of public planning processes, in conjunction with guided recovery programs. Too often, remediation programs are seen as the result of economic and engineering studies, but first comes the creation of public awareness and a will for action that can best be developed by public planning activities.

Environmental Quality Competition

One of the surest ways to achieve environmental best management practices in tourism activities is to seek ways to introduce competition based on relevant quality measures. Directorate XXIII of the Commission of the European Community produced a study of the environmental effects of tourism throughout the European Community which recommends regional programs to stimulate "environmental competition" among states and destinations of the continent. This concept should be adopted to those areas already most dependent on tourism.

There are several elements to such a strategy. One excellent model for this at the regional level would be adaptation of the Blue Flag program which has been developed by UNEP, the World Tourism Organization and the Foundation for Environmental Education in Europe, to certify the environmental quality of beaches throughout Europe.

Assessments of Facilities

To achieve environmental best management practices for tourism requires improved information use and information sharing about environmental conditions in coastal areas. The development of tourism facilities of environmental quality is a collaborative process involving developers, local communities, and national authorities. National authorities have a three-part role in this process:

— managing the relationship with the local community,

— weighing and approving the development proposal, and

— providing background information about conditions at the development site.

National governments should organize information on "developable" sites as part of the national resource inventory and information base, with a view to providing both local communities and developers with the most complete picture possible on environmental conditions. Specifically, as part of the national coastal management programs, monitoring data and assessment information for key coastal areas should be catalogued and assembled in one place to support the assessment of trends and to provide baseline data for development proposals and construction impacts monitoring. The use of Environmental Impact Assessments for major tourism projects is well established throughout the world. Systematic collection of environmental data about key sites is an especially useful extension of this process, permitting better assessments by developers and their environmental consultants, and the application of more objective review standards by government agencies.

Quality Improvement

Within the past decade the so-called "quality movement" has achieved major international recognition with the establishment of international standards for documenting management and quality concerns. This activity has been coordinated by the European-based International Organization for Standardization (ISO), and resulted in the ISO 9000 series of standards for quality management. This standard provides a process by which a firm may be certified as complying with relevant management and quality auditing considerations, across all international boundaries. Therefore a German purchaser of goods and services from a Japanese-based tractor manufacturer certified as meeting ISO-9000 standards, for example, can be assured that these tractors must meet the same strict standards as similarly certified German or Canadian producers.

Although there are limited environmental components to the ISO-9000 standards, beginning in 1991, ISO set up Technical Committee 207 to work on standards for Environmental Management Standards (EMS) and environmental auditing. Draft versions of the general Environmental Management Standards have been published, but this is only the first phase in a process which includes four work groups for Environmental Auditing, three work groups for Environmental Labeling, two for Environmental Performance Evaluation, and five work groups for Life Cycle Analysis.

Perhaps most significantly, the ISO 14000 process requires setting sector-specific guidelines or guidance standards. Countries should study the development and publication of guidance for tourism, in order to assure that the special environmental conditions of the region are covered by all of the guidance terms. By studying the certification standards of ISO 14000, countries will be able to secure guidance for information and reporting standards that developers should be expected to apply to tourism developments. Especially for development or management of major tourism facilities, national authorities should require firms to meet ISO 14000 certification standards to be able to participate in development and management of the project.

Training and Operating Standards

Operation of tourism facilities is a major management practice with multiple environmental consequences. Countries should work closely with major tourism facilities on the planning and implementation of operating training processes:

— To ensure that training and operating systems meet acceptable standards that reflect local priorities and conditions; and,

— To work with the leaders of the industry to find ways to provide similar levels of training for staff and operators of smaller facilities, such as small hotels, marinas, taxis, restaurants and guest houses.

In countries which maintain tourism training programs, such a system should be integrated with the industry's training efforts, and on-the-job training provided by operating facilities should be coordinated with and complementary to training schools. The Green Globe tourism training and management program of the World Tourism and Travel Council and UNEP is an important resource in training service workers in the tourist industry.

Role of Government in Coastal Tourism Management

As an economic activity, tourism is difficult to influence and manage directly. Like most coastal development in market economies, tourism-related development is driven largely by the private sector and its assessment of economic opportunities. Miller and Auyong point out that tourism involves mainly three sets of actors: tourists, locals, and two categories of brokers.

Tourism tends to be globally driven by market forces influenced by such factors as advertising (by public or private agents at the tourist destination), the perceptions of the traveling public about security, amenity values, etc., and, in the case of international tourists, by currency factors. Notwithstanding these difficulties, there is much that the federal government, working with the states and localities, does to ensure that coastal tourism is conducted in a sustainable manner, thereby ensuring long term economic and environmental benefits for coastal communities and the nation. Sustainable development of coastal tourism is dependent on:

1. good coastal management practices (particularly regarding proper siting of tourism infrastructure and the provision of public access);
2. clean water and air, and healthy coastal ecosystems;
3. maintaining a safe and secure recreational environment though the management of coastal hazards (such as erosion, storms, floods), and the provision of adequate levels of safety for boaters, swimmers, and other water users;
4. beach restoration efforts that maintain the recreational and amenity values of beaches; and,
5. sound policies for wildlife and habitat protection.

While there are separate federal programs dealing with each of these areas, some more successfully than others, in recent years there has been a growing realization among a number of federal agencies that these factors are interconnected and that all are needed to achieve healthy ecosystems and sustainable economies in coastal communities.

6

Beach Management

Beach management seeks to maintain or improve a beach as a recreational resource and a means of coast protection, while providing facilities that meet the needs and aspirations of those who use the beach. It includes the framing and policing of any necessary regulations, and decisions on the design and location of any structures needed to facilitate the use and enjoyment of the beach environment. In most countries, a single "beach manager" who undertakes all the activities such as monitoring, planning and decision-making does not exist. These activities are generally devolved among different persons and authorities at various levels (national, federal, regional, provincial, local).

In order to achieve effective management of recreational water use areas, managers should have background knowledge on a range of aspects concerned with the coastal or freshwater area, such as inflows and outflows, water quality, physical aspects of the water use area and potential health hazards. Beach managers should, therefore, be aware of the social and economic dimension embedded in their decision-making. Of importance to beach managers and decision-makers are:

— The techniques available to measure the impact of tourism.

- Notions and principles of sustainability.
- Local strategies towards sustainability.
- Sustainability indicators and issues related to water quality management.
- Water analysis and water safety.

The coastal zone and freshwater bodies are important areas for human habitation, industry and recreation. There are thus competing uses, not only of water for bathing, surfing, sailing, scuba diving, aquaculture and other maritime industries, but also of land use, such as for residential developments, harbours, ports, marinas and tourism industries. Offshore activities such as oil and gas exploration, disposal of sewage or radioactive waste and shipping, are also responsible for the release of contaminants into the aquatic environments.

Many of the pressures mentioned above are common throughout the world and many of the threats facing the quality of recreational water bodies have arisen as a direct or indirect consequence of human activities. Such conflict of uses makes management of recreational water use areas a particular challenge. Water bodies are often used as a repository for waste and the relatively concentrated period of tourism activity in specific areas increases the environmental pressures on such water bodies. Recreational use of water and tourism activities depend highly on the quality of the natural environment for their continued success. Lack of effective management can lead to the loss of habitats, over exploitation of resources and an associated loss of income.

The coastline is a major element in the geographic, recreational, commercial and ecological fabric of many countries and provides major destinations for local, national and international tourists. Freshwater areas, such as large lakes, are popular for recreation and in many cases are being developed for tourism. Associated villages and towns grow and develop their economy in accordance with the prevailing and seasonal tourism needs (main commercial streets, hotels, restaurants, clubs, shops and related activities; recreational activities on the beach or on lakes; transportation facilities, etc.).

Socio-economic problems usually derive from the seasonality of the pressures on tourism-related facilities. There are a few data available on the contribution of coastal zone tourism to national economies but for smaller coastal countries and island countries, especially those without industrial or agricultural outputs, tourism can be a substantial part of the economy.

There are concerns associated with the development of touristic ventures that can apply to both marine and freshwater areas. These concerns include tourism-associated aquatic transportation and the resulting pollution from vessels (oil, tar or litter on the adjacent area), as well as stress on populations and the environment where tourism is the major factor in the economy.

The development of tourist facilities may have a particular effect in developing countries where food security problems, pressures from recreational lobbies and public opinion may threaten alternative sources of income, such as the local fishery economy. Mariculture and the recovery of oil and gas can compete for the same space as that desired by recreational users.

Tourists themselves can contribute to the waste and pollution of the host area, with a degrading influence on the quality of the recreational water use area arising from noise (primarily from transportation), recreational activities such as boating, and from solid and liquid wastes. Biodiversity reduction, resource depletion and human health problems may result from the accumulated environmental effects of tourism, including direct human impact (such as trampling).

There are a number of issues that may deter tourists from a recreational water use area. These include aesthetic and health problems arising from domestic waste disposal into marine and freshwaters that jeopardises the quality of food and the possibility of recreational activities on beaches in developing and developed nations. Eutrophication can degrade beaches and adjacent waters aesthetically through the accumulation of rotting marine plants; this can lead to a significant loss in tourist revenue. Aesthetic factors, such as litter, have a high deterrent value on visitors to bathing water areas.

Integrated coastal zone management (ICZM) is understood most simply as management of the coastal zone as a whole in relation to local, regional, national and international goals. It implies a focus on the interactions between the various activities and resource demands that occur within the coastal zone, and between coastal zone activities and activities in other regions. This might mean, for example, the incorporation of coastal environment protection goals into economic and technical decision-making processes or the co-ordination of tourism policies with nature conservation policies.

Although ICZM has been promoted widely in recent years, it has not always been implemented successfully. This was mainly because of a lack of understanding of underlying coastal processes and it has only become apparent relatively recently that multidisciplinary land-use planning in the coastal zone is essential. Financial constraints have also been a contributory factor. The same principles of ICZM can be applied to freshwater management and therefore marine and freshwater zones will be treated as synonymous in this chapter. In general, recreational water use areas, whether fresh or coastal waters, require similar management actions. However, lakes and other freshwater recreational water use areas are generally smaller bodies of water and are, by nature, more fragile than seas and oceans. The impact of human activities are apparent more quickly and failure to ensure adequate management will accentuate any degradation.

Integrated coastal zone management programmes must address a range of issues, including habitat (loss of habitat or degradation of coral reefs, seagrass beds, wetlands, beaches and dunes, lagoons and estuaries), water quality (sources and nature of pollution, reduction and flow rates); management of natural hazards, and degradation of cultural resources and management of developments (mariculture, extractive industries, tourism, shore front development, major facility siting). Coastal managers must also consider any decline in fisheries, public access, biodiversity protection, sea level rise and degradation of scenic quality.

Integrated management ensures that priorities are given to all users of the water zone. Through policy supported by legislation and regulations, the most appropriate activity or activities can be given preference and investments in the area can concentrate selectively on these activities. Funding is a common problem in environmental management and for this reason some form of classification scheme combining priority for action and type of action required is especially useful. The classification then becomes an important tool in assisting planners in developing a strategy for improving the quality of the bathing water and the beaches. When the problem can be rectified through local efforts (such as beach cleaning), the management process should seek appropriate action from the municipality and reclassify the beach accordingly. Where the cause requires major investments or decisions on regional or perhaps national level, the authority should ensure that health concerns are represented adequately.

It is important to emphasise that improving the bathing water and beach quality strictly with the purpose of increasing the amount of tourists visiting a region or a country, can conflict with interests in protecting ecologically important areas or designated sensitive areas, etc. It must be an important issue for planners at regional, as well as national level to develop a plan for selecting and protecting these areas that are not to be transformed into large intensive tourist resorts. This is a premise for working with a classification scheme.

Management Framework

The WHO Guidelines for Safe Recreational-water Environments present a management framework within which different levels of health risk and associated interventions are ordered in four major fields under the umbrella of integrated management. The major fields of intervention are clustered as regulatory compliance, public awareness and information, control and abatement technology, and public health advice and intervention.

Legislation and Regulation

Effective coastal or freshwater zone management requires an effective legislative framework to define the roles of different bodies and levels of government, as well as to provide environmental objectives. Management is not restricted to national issues - water quality, pollution control, international tourism and shipping are amongst the activities that affect the coastal zone and that extend beyond the national boundary. It is therefore obvious that a single government or agency cannot be responsible for the wide range of issues that need to be addressed in the coastal or freshwater zone. Effective legislation must provide a framework within which the roles and responsibilities of different organisations or interested groups are defined and must accommodate capacity to act at the international, national and local levels.

At an international level, legislation of particular relevance often relates to the management of international or transboundary waters. Whilst the legislation itself may be "hard law" or "soft law", it may provide for harmonisation or standardisation in data generation and exchange, and create obligations to notify other concerned parties regarding hazards and quality changes.

At a national level, regulatory measures are often considered to be inflexible but they are easy to operate and provide a clear and common framework for all parties concerned. In general, some form of basic water law provides a framework within which specified agencies are empowered to regulate. In the field of recreational water use, the national level is particularly important in establishing common ground for the assessment and reporting of safety and thereby supporting "informed personal choice". However, laws and regulations of relevance to safe beach management may derive from diverse influences, such as public health, social integration and rights of the disabled people, navigation for pleasure purposes, aquatic sports, fishing activities (in the sea and on the shore, e.g. bivalves), relevant flying activities, trade activities on public areas and the concession of State lands.

The diversity of national regulatory structures requires diverse approaches and solutions but, in general, managers concerned with recreational water use areas should consider both common law and statutory law. In most countries under common law, liability and negligence arise from the breach of duty known as "duty of care". This applies to members of the public as well as to operators. The duty specified is to take reasonable care. In the case of the safe management of the beach, the responsibility for taking adequate precautions rests with the operator. Of particular importance to those concerned with beach operation is the standard of care arising from their activities, i.e. that of an ordinary skilled person exercising or professing to have a particular skill. This is of particular relevance to lifeguards, for example, who are expected to conduct themselves as one would expect of the competent qualified lifeguard.

Those who employ staff on a beach may have specific duties to those staff under statutory law. In general these duties cover premises, written operating procedures, general working conditions, training, appropriate health and safety policy statements, consultation with safety representatives, safety procedures, the free provision of appropriate uniform, protective clothing and personal safety equipment and the provision of adequate first aid facilities for employees. For the employers there is an obligation to conduct operations in such a way as to ensure that members of the public are not exposed to risks to their health and safety.

The occupier of premises has a duty of care to any visitor using the premises for the purpose for which he is invited or permitted to be there. In general the operator of a natural beach will not be exposed to liability, although only one attraction, such as a diving platform, would expose the operator to liability if the duty of care is breached. The same applies to any operator deriving income from the provision of services for visiting swimmers. The operator may be exonerated from liability if a danger is brought to the visitors' attention and the operator takes appropriate measures.

Public Awareness

The concept of reciprocal rights and responsibilities (as implicit in the concept of duty of care) highlights the importance of the capacity of the individual to make healthy or safe choices. In order to participate successfully in healthy recreation, members of the public require awareness (i.e. in this context knowledge regarding hazards and safe behaviours) and access to information to enable them to make informed choices. However, informed personal choice contributes not only to the protection of the individual but creates an incentive for improvement in the quality and safety of recreational water use areas - as users demand safer locations, the economic incentive to provide safe and attractive facilities increases.

A basic appreciation of the health hazards that may be encountered during recreational water use and regarding safe behaviours is a prerequisite to health protection through the exercise of improved personal choice. A variety of special interest groups, such as lifeguard organisations, are instrumental in promoting education and public awareness activities. Watersport clubs, such as sailing, scuba diving, canoeing and swimming clubs, teach members basic first aid, safety procedures and a respect for the water environment. All watersports are potentially hazardous and participants should be made aware of the particular hazards associated with their sport. A variety of formal courses, usually culminating in an examination, are in existence to ensure that such activities are undertaken in a safe and responsible manner.

Beach Classification

One tool to support informed personal choice that has received great attention in recent years is that of beach classification. In order to be effective a beach classification scheme needs to be based upon health and safety and must be of interest to users. It must also be based on reliable comparable data and overseen by a credible and impartial agency. Whilst classification schemes are often designed specifically to support and encourage informed personal choice, other classification schemes may be used for purely management information purposes, such as for determining beaches inappropriate for tourism development, or for identifying those suitable for the encouragement of tourism and perhaps those eligible for certain forms of aid or awards from a national or regional authority.

In order to decide to which class a beach belongs, certain criteria for each class need to be defined. A classification system allows differences between classes to express differences in the problems to be solved. This means that different programmes or plans are needed depending on what class a specific recreational water use area belongs to. It also implies that the classification of beaches and water is a continuous process. A certain beach or water may belong to one class in one year, but as different measures are taken and problems are solved, the beach or water may change class next year.

On-site and Local Information

Users of recreational water use areas rely on information about safety, hazards to health and facilities, that comes from the news media, local authority notice boards and signs, environmental groups and tourist publicity, as well as relying on their own perceptions. Users can only control risks actively by acting on knowledge provided to them. Public awareness measures at the local level, in combination with national policies, are thus essential in order to achieve effective management of the recreational water use area and to reduce risks to users.

Control and Abatement Technology

Not all hazards encountered during recreational use of the water environment may be addressed effectively, or their associated adverse health effects averted, through informed personal choice. In some instances removal of the hazard or preventing access to the hazard is the preferred management option. In precluding access to a hazard high intervention approaches (such as fencing) or low intervention such as making access difficult (no development of car parks or public transport access), can be used. Such measures are relevant to a range of hazards, such as areas with strong currents, rocky environments, poor water quality or areas subject to toxic cyanobacterial blooms. To achieve long-term improvements in the quality of recreational waters investment must be made in pollution abatement technologies.

Public Health Intervention

Despite concern for the aesthetic aspects of recreational water use areas, the driving force behind much activity is public health and safety. In many cases circumstances may lead to situations that present an unfamiliar or unacceptable risk to public health. Such circumstances may relate to a breakdown in sewage treatment and disposal infrastructure, to toxic cyanobacterial blooms or to new or transient water uses that are incompatible with existing patterns of use. Under such circumstances the authorities responsible for public health are generally required to take a lead role in determining what actions should be taken and for what period. Such decisions are, in practice, often made under pressure of time and with inadequate information, but may be assisted by the existence of a national point of reference where experience and information on such incidents is maintained.

In addition to emergency response, some countries have, in recent years, instigated some form of accident emergency plans. These deal with, for example, major oil accidents at sea, or a chemical industry or nuclear accident. A structure for alert systems or notification relays, including home numbers for authority staff, may already exist. Unfortunately, the more common pollution accidents, such as failure of a sewage treatment plant or unusual wind direction forcing polluted waters onto a beach which is normally clean, or an algal bloom causing skin irritation, are often not included in this system. They do, however, affect the public more directly. It is therefore preferable to establish warning systems for these kind of events.

Beaches with a full lifeguard or warden service have most of an alert system in place, i.e. a dedicated person with warning signals on site during the bathing season. However, lifeguards are often only responsible for alerting the public to specific hazards, such as high winds, and not to pollution incidents, although in reality they, along with other coastal workers (e.g. rangers, wardens or coastguards) would alert the public to such incidents.

Role of Organisations and Individuals

The large number of interested organisations at all levels involved in the coastal and freshwater zones requires particular co-ordination and co-operation. Central and local governments have a particular responsibility to establish standards and regulations to limit the health hazards to users of recreational water environments. Of particular importance is the layout of a management strategy for the achievement of integrated management. This requires addressing the issues of resources, economic development activities and societal needs in recreational water use areas.

National government is also instrumental in directing, promoting and co-ordinating all activities relating to the application of laws concerning the coastal zone, including defining general criteria and methodologies for the monitoring of recreational water environments and activities, mode and frequency of sampling and analytical techniques. Organisations such as the World Health Organization Advisory Committee on the Protection of the Sea and other such bodies can provide advice and guidance.

Research institutions, universities, non-governmental organisations (NGOs), special interest groups and the tourism industry can aid in the technical assessment of hazards and in monitoring changes. Industry, in particular the tourism industry, is increasingly adopting a more proactive role in monitoring the environment. Local interest groups, NGOs, local authorities, the tourism industry and the media are involved in raising awareness of users to some of the hazards associated with recreational activities. Citizens are often instrumental in contributing to remedial measures and are increasingly involved in public participation activities, such as beach cleaning, riverine fly tipping area cleanups and monitoring.

Local Authorities

Local authorities are frequently the legal agency of the government. They often take a key role in bringing interested organisations together and gaining their collaboration and co-operation in decision-making, and participation in the implementation of decisions. Local authorities also contribute to the development and enforcement of standards and regulations. In general, public health laws and acts state that a local authority may make bylaws with respect to public bathing and beach management, including public bathing and coastal zone management.

Municipalities may therefore be responsible for regulation of the areas and the hours when bathing will be permitted; they may also be responsible for requiring the persons providing accommodation for bathing to provide and maintain lifesaving appliances and lifeguards, as well as being responsible for the regulations for preventing danger to bathers. Municipalities may also enforce regulations regarding the navigation and speed of vehicles for pleasure purposes within any area allotted for public bathing. This is of particular importance because it permits the zoning of pleasure vehicles in relation to bathers.

Municipalities may also be responsible for all the inland and adjacent areas above the low water mark where these bylaws have affect; protection of public health and safety, including monitoring of water and adjacent land. Protection, preservation, restoration and enhancement of coastal natural resources (including beaches, floodplains and dunes) as well as the use of beachfront property in a manner compatible with preserving public property may be the responsibility of the municipality.

Municipalities may be required to produce coastline management plans as part of their normal planning responsibilities and any local authority with land subject to coastline hazards should plan and manage that land in accordance with its hazard susceptibility. Local authorities are therefore responsible for the investigation, design, construction and maintenance of works and measures to mitigate coastline hazards and also for promoting hazard awareness in their community in an attempt to reduce the social disruption and damage caused by coastline hazards. The latter can be done by supplying information and advice to property owners, residents, visitors, potential purchasers and investors. It is also a local authority responsibility to improve and maintain beaches and their amenity.

The structure and responsibilities of local governments differ throughout the world. In the UK, for example, County Councils are responsible for strategic planning, structure plans and waste disposal and the District Councils are responsible for housing, local planning, environmental health, coast protection, waste collection and noise control.

In Australia, the Local Councils have general responsibilities for the production of coastline management plans, coastline hazard mitigation, hazard awareness and beach management, as well as specific responsibilities under the Environmental Planning and Assessment Act. In general, however, the fragmented and often duplicated responsibilities in the coastal zone are identified as severe impediments to effective planning and management.

Facility Operators

Once a beach manager has a complete picture of the beach characteristics (beach registration and classification) all decision elements are available for the daily operation of the beach and for (mid- to long-term) management plans. It is suggested that the competent authority should designate an operator, or another responsible person, to be on duty when a beach is open for visitors. This operator should take decisions relating to the beach and should take appropriate action when requested by the authority when accidents or spills take place leading to beach contamination or when water quality becomes unacceptable or for safety reasons (such as weather, inadequate lifeguards or safety equipment).

There are also a number of considerations to take into account when designing the facilities to support a public beach. Resources become an important issue and therefore the provision of facilities should be prioritised according to the needs and uses of the area under question. Monitoring for potential health hazards and associated management actions should always be considered a priority over the provision of shops and refreshment kiosks when developing recreational water use areas.

However, it is acknowledged that this approach would not always attract tourists and the associated finance to an area. Research has shown that visitors to the coastline place more value on the cleanliness of an area and on the provision of facilities than on unseen human health hazards such as microbiological parameters. Education and public awareness must, therefore, become an essential part of integrated management, especially where resources are low and prohibit the provision of facilities. Consultation between those with a vested interest and local communities is essential if the various conflicts of use are to be resolved.

Management Options

The various different attitudes of visitors to the recreational water use area also determine the necessary level of facilities that are desired. Different cultural contrasts exist in the use of beaches; in many tropical areas the sea is used as a cleaning place or for trade amongst fishermen, whereas throughout Europe beaches are generally used as places of passive activity. Despite many people looking for seclusion at a beach, the pressures to develop recreational water use areas to support growing populations and increases in tourism are so great that it is becoming very difficult to find underdeveloped beaches, particularly in countries with a warm climate.

Management options and preferences vary according to the level of development of an area and the preferences of visitors to that area. Management actions need to take into account local economic needs as well as the desires of the users. In general, two broad categories of user can be identified: those seeking resort areas with facilities, entertainment and easy access, and those seeking secluded or rural areas.

Resort Beaches

Where resources are a restraining factor careful prioritisation should occur that will minimise public health risks. Topography, including slope and bottom material, need to be considered. Beach cleaning should also address the removal of litter and debris from the lake or seabed where they present a hazard to bathers. Specific regulations may be adopted for the prohibition of potentially hazardous items, such as glass, on the beaches. In addition, adequate litter bins should be provided.

Clearly visible depth markers should be provided at the points of maximum depth of all designated areas and at diving boards, platforms and similar facilities. Zoning is an important measure in minimising risk where different user groups coexist within a confined area (i.e. dog-free zones, conservation areas and naturist zones, zones for swimming, sailboarding, powerboating, etc.). Swimming may be limited to a specific area, i.e. the least hazardous, which also facilitates supervision and segregation of incompatible activities.

Wastewater from toilets and showers should be discharged to the local municipal sewage system. If that is not possible an alternative treatment should be established that is acceptable to local or national standards. Where possible, toilet facilities and showers should be provided in adequate number. To prevent cars and vehicles driving on the beach, access facilities should be provided to beach parking areas.

Access to beach areas for emergency vehicles should be provided and appropriately signposted. Easily read and understood information boards should be used to display beach regulations, general information on beach and water quality and facilities. The signs should be located so that they will be seen at the access points before entering the beach, the resort or the swimming area. Where appropriate, more formal regulations, in the form of bylaws, may be adopted to control activities at the coastal zone, particularly noise, fires, dog fouling and litter.

Safety aspects are of particular importance to coastal managers of tourist beaches. Clearly identified warning signs should be provided where appropriate indicating, for example, when the beach is closed for swimming, the times when lifeguards are on duty, danger of swimming during heavy storms or after sunset or in dangerous currents.

Rural Beaches

Ideally, as with resort beaches, rural beaches should be monitored for potential health risks as a priority. Rural beaches are generally popular with walkers, naturalists, and fishermen and for other kinds of casual enjoyment. Such beaches should be cleaned "as needed" but at least four times a year. Beaches that are particularly frequently used shall be cleaned at least once a week during the summer and each month during the winter.

On rural beaches, safety boards should be displayed at all principal access points to beaches, in car parks (if present) and at particular hazard spots. The hazards of the particular beach should be clearly indicated, together with the times of high and low water, the distance of the nearest telephone and some useful telephone numbers, and the location of the nearest first aid facilities. It is suggested that public rescue equipment should also be in place in the more frequented rural beaches.

Elements of Good Practice

— The management framework developed for a bathing water area must take into account the impact of various competing activities, sustainable management processes, water quality issues and associated safety issues.

— Such a framework must reconcile development pressures with socio-economic, cultural and environmental criteria.

— The full range of legislative and regulatory controls that interplay with coastal or freshwater recreational water management must be incorporated into the management framework including duty of care, health and safety legislation, water quality regulations, pollution control and international articles governing international tourism and shipping. Such measures will vary from local bylaws through national to international law.

— The development of an integrated management framework must include a range of issues including nature conservation, water quality, management of coastal development access and environmental degradation.

— The role of a local municipality is central to an effective coastal management framework. Their activities must be co-ordinated within a coherent national context.

— A beach classification scheme can be constructed which provides a discreet hierarchy of categories and concomitant management activities.

— On completion of a full catalogue of the characteristics of a particular recreational water area, the beach manager has the framework from within which to establish the operational activity.

Beach Restoration Programs

The governments have long played an important role in the maintenance and restoration of the nation's beaches and shores. Experience in shore protection efforts has shown that soft solutions involving beach re-nourishment have produced better, more economical results than hard solutions such as seawalls and groins in many circumstances.

Seawalls and revetments first developed as the field of coastal engineering emerged. While these measures are often successful at protecting the development and infrastructure behind a beach, they do not address the real cause of beach erosion, which is a lack of sediment in the system. As understanding of coastal systems has grown through research and data collection programs, solutions to such problems has progressed. Today, beach re-nourishment represents a sound engineering solution that is economically feasible and environmentally sensitive. Only in areas with very high erosion rates and substantial shoreside facilities to protect are hard structural solutions considered.

The shift of population to coastal counties and the increased demand for coastal tourism destinations has exacerbated many existing beach erosion problems. Development in areas with high erosion rates and building on or in front of sand dunes, rather than behind them, are major factors contributing to increased beach erosion problems. Relative sea-level rise caused primarily by subsidence is another major factor in some areas. The interruption of sand flowing along the coast by natural or stabilized inlets is also an aggravating factor.

Given the role played by beach tourism in the nations' balance of payments and its impact on government revenues and regional and local economies, it is crucial that these assets be maintained at levels that promote and enhance their recreational use. If budgetary constraints make it necessary to reduce federal assistance for beach restoration and maintenance, a gradual and predictable approach should be adopted and states and coastal communities assisted in developing viable alternative funding arrangements.

Any one, be it poorly planned development, poor coastal water quality, unsafe or hazardous conditions, or eroding beaches, could seriously impact the tourism potential of a coastal area. Furthermore, policies and programs in each of these areas need to be developed and implemented in an integrated fashion, each taking account of the others. Failure to do this can result in such undesirable outcomes as erosion control structures that impair the recreational experience, or poorly designed development that causes water pollution or beach erosion.

Strategies for Beach Monitoring

The key elements of a beach monitoring programme include the following:

a) The beach monitoring programmes should be maintained and expanded to include other parameters.

b) Information flow between government departments needs to be improved; inter-agency committees are the proposed mechanism.

c) Increased work in awareness is required to ensure that all groups, especially senior administrators and politicians, have a better understanding of the various issues relating to beach management.

d) Beach resources and their management needs to be brought into the classroom at the primary and secondary level.

e) Existing coastal development setbacks need to be reviewed with a view to establishing variable setbacks for beaches in each island.

f) Legislative review of existing beach protection laws is necessary.

g) Enforcement is one of the weakest areas of beach management. Its success requires that the socio-cultural aspects of beach management be addressed at the community and national level, so that local residents can police their natural resources. Greater cooperation between enforcement agencies is also required at the national level.

In order to achieve effective coastal area management, there is a need for greater cooperation and collaboration at the local, national, regional and international levels.Acceptable change and change thresholds during the construction and operation of the proposed project to ensure that major changes in function and relationships have been fully considered in the planning and approval process. In addition, site planning requires the monitoring of both baseline and in-process changes in environmental activities. This often requires a slower rate of construction than contractors could accomplish if they were free to ignore environmental impacts and mitigation strategies.

Other steps in a sustainable site and building planning process include:

— Model the ecosystem;

— Assess social and economic conditions;

— Establish the acceptable limits of change and the phases for re-evaluation of impacts and re-design;

— Design the facility within social and environmental limits;

— Monitor site conditions throughout construction;

— Re-evaluate during construction or between construction phases

Sustainable building design is an extension of the site design concepts, beginning with orientation to the site itself. Sustainable building design also requires an attempt to balance human needs with the limits on acceptable change for the site. Sustainable building design must:

— reflect ecosystem and cultural conditions, rather than imposing new values on them;

— stress support for environmental responsiveness and regeneration, rather than creating new environmental communities;

— focus attention on and appreciation for the natural conditions of the site;

— avoid the use of energy-intensive or environmentally damaging materials or operations; and

— focus on adaptive use of existing resources to save costs and stress in the construction process.

Priority natural factors which the building design needs to address include: climate, vegetation, topography, water bodies, hydrology, geology and soils, natural hazards, and pests and wildlife.

A discussion of best management practices for tourism planning and design issues must also acknowledge that best management practices for coastal tourism are a special case of the general need for integrated coastal area planning and management processes, with all of the problems of jurisdictional conflict and potentially overlapping policy objectives that implies.

In jurisdictions with a high dependence on tourism, the high profile of tourism development can be used to showcase and support other good management practices. In areas with less prominent tourism, coastal tourism management practices should be developed directly as components of the wider coastal area management plan.

7

Biological, Physical and Chemical Hazards

There are a number of other diverse biological, physical and chemical hazards that could be encountered in the recreational water environment. Many of these are local in nature and should be addressed in monitoring programmes where they are known or suspected to be locally important. The characteristics of the hazard and the local conditions define the appropriate remedial measures. It is important that standards, monitoring and implementation enable preventative and remedial actions in this time frame that will prevent health effects arising from such hazards. The WHO Guidelines for Safe Recreational-water Environments emphasise the importance of identification of circumstances that will support a continuously safe environment for recreation.

Biological Hazards

Injuries from dangerous aquatic organisms may be sustained in a number of ways, for example accidental encounters with venomous sessile or floating organisms when bathing or treading on stingrays, weeverfish or sea urchins.Unnecessary handling, or provocation of venomous organisms during seashore exploration, or invading the territory of animals when swimming may also lead to injury.

Routine monitoring for biological hazards is justified only where they exist. Monitoring should respond to local conditions; for example where there is a known hazard, such as jellyfish, it is important to identify the source and the nature of the hazard.

Many serious incidents can be avoided through an increase in public education and awareness. Surveillance systems should be in place to provide warnings to the public in areas where it is known that sharks, jellyfish and other hazardous organisms are common. It is important to identify and to assess the risks from various aquatic organisms in a given region. Where the health outcomes are known to be mild, remedial measures should be based primarily upon raising public awareness and providing information to the public. This may be done in a number of ways and may require only simple messages, such as advice to wear suitable footwear whilst exploring the intertidal area or to avoid handling marine or freshwater organisms. Where the health outcomes are known to be more severe it may be necessary to declare exclusion zones in bathing areas or to restrict bathing where or when appropriate.

Microbiological hazards

Leptospirosis

Leptospirosis is usually characterised by the sudden onset of fever and chills, severe headache, muscular pain, abdominal pain, nausea and conjunctivitis. The causative bacterium is of the genus Leptospira. Other symptoms may include aseptic meningitis, conjunctival haemorrhage, rash, jaundice and cough with bloodstained sputum. The organism enters the body either through abraded skin or by contact with mucous membranes. The incubation period is 10-12 days and symptoms persist for approximately one week. Prolonged mental health symptoms may occur after leptospirosis but the relationship is not well documented.

Water becomes contaminated with leptospires from the urine of infected domestic animals and rodents. Therefore, the common faecal indicator organisms cannot be relied upon as indicators of the presence of the Leptospira. The detection of pathogenic leptospires in water is difficult. They are relatively slow growing during enrichment and do not compete well against other more rapid growing organisms. Culture reactions and serology are required to distinguish pathogenic and saprophytic strains.

Routine monitoring is not recommended but recreational waters should be examined for leptospires when they are suspected to be the source of an outbreak of leptospirosis. For example, a recent outbreak of leptospirosis following a triathlon race in Springfield, USA, clearly illustrated the need for monitoring, particularly where large numbers of people are at risk.

The risk of leptospirosis can be reduced by preventing direct animal access to swimming areas, by treating farm animal wastes prior to discharge and by informing users about the risks of swimming in water that is accessible to domestic and wild animals. Outbreaks of the disease are not common and the risk of leptospirosis associated with swimming areas is low. Outbreaks associated with salt water have never been reported. As a precautionary measure, domestic and wild animals should not have access to swimming areas.

Schistosomes

Among human parasitic diseases, schistosomiasis

(sometimes called bilharziasis) ranks second behind malaria in terms of socio-economic impact and health consequences in tropical and subtropical areas. The disease is endemic in 74 developing countries and world-wide some 200 million people are infected.

The major forms of schistosomiasis are caused by five species of water-borne flatworms, or blood flukes, called schistosomes. Humans become infected after contact with water containing the infective stage of the parasite. Intestinal schistosomiasis caused by Schistosoma mansoni occurs in the Eastern Mediterranean, Sub Saharan Africa, the Caribbean and South America. Oriental or Asiatic intestinal schistosomiasis, caused by the S. japonicum group of parasites, is endemic in South East Asia and in the Western Pacific region. Another species of S. intercalatum has been reported from 10 African countries. Urinary schistosomiasis, caused by S. haematobium, is endemic in Africa and the Eastern Mediterranean. Each of the five species may give rise to acute or chronic disease with widely differing symptoms and clinical signs.

A computerised global database for schistosomiasis has been established by WHO. The database includes information on epidemiology, control activities, people responsible for control, and water resources for each endemic country.

Schistosomiasis and water are inextricably linked and the high prevalence of schistosomiasis in many parts of the world is closely related to human contact with natural water bodies. Some water contact is occupational and to some extent necessary, but most transmission of schistosomiasis occurs during water contact for domestic and recreational purposes. In endemic areas used by local populations or tourists, monitoring programmes should be implemented. Health education, information and communication are therefore important in a strategy to control morbidity. The objectives of health education are to help people understand that their own behaviour, principally water use practices and indiscriminate urination and defecation, as well as failure to use available screening services or to comply with medical treatment, is a key factor in transmission.

In the short term, where the prevalence of schistosomiasis is high, population-based chemotherapy can reduce the prevalence, severity and morbidity of the disease. Long-term operational and budgetary planning should be made for diagnostic facilities and re-treatment schedules, as well as treatment throughout the health care system and for transmission control. In areas where tourism is important to the economy, molluscides (chemicals that kill the aquatic intermediate host snails) may be applied at specific locations. However, molluscicides are expensive and have impacts on other aquatic life.

Heat and Cold

Prolonged recreational use of water can lead to exposure to extreme cold or excessive solar radiation. Staying on the adjacent land area can also lead to enhanced exposure to ultraviolet (UV) radiation, because of the reflection of the sun's rays from the surface of the water. Children are often more at risk because they tend not to use sunglasses and because they spend long periods of time going in and out of the water without a protective sunscreen.

Skin cancers and cataracts are important health concerns - the United Nations Environment Programme (UNEP) has estimated that over 2 × 106 non-melanoma skin cancers and 200,000 malignant melanomas occur globally each year. It has been reported by WHO that over half of the world's blind population lose their eyesight because of cataract. It is believed that in about 20 per cent of cataract sufferers disease is triggered by short wave ultraviolet light. Direct exposure to UV radiation has both harmful and beneficial effects on humans.

A number of epidemiological studies have implicated solar radiation as a cause of skin cancer in fair-skinned humans and severe sunburn in children has been shown as a risk factor for malignant melanoma.

Severe heat stress is also a potential risk for anyone exposed to high temperatures. The most common clinical syndromes are heat cramps, heat exhaustion and heat stroke. Recreational water users commonly expose themselves to prolonged periods of high temperatures, which is often exacerbated if they are undergoing physical exercise.

Exposure to extreme low temperatures, such as often experienced by swimmers in the open sea can also present health risks. When the body temperature falls there is a sense of confusion, a reduction in swimming capability (coupled with an overestimation of swimming capability), a possible loss of consciousness, and death by hypothermic cardiac arrest or drowning.

Health education campaigns play an important part in the prevention of health effects due to sun, heat and cold exposure. In the UK, for example, 89 per cent of health authorities were found by Sabri and Harvey to be implementing primary prevention programmes in an attempt to meet the Government's "Health of the Nation" target of stabilising incidence of skin cancer by the year 2005.

However, relatively few of these prevention programmes have been evaluated. Data from Australia have shown that the "Slip! Slop! Slap!" campaign that was initiated in 1980, and its follow-up campaign "Sunsmart" in 1988, were effective in increasing awareness and self-reported sun-protection behaviour.

Evaluation of other health education campaigns in various countries have reported improved public knowledge about the dangers of exposure to sunshine but no significant change in sun-protection behaviour. Where a corresponding change in behaviour was reported, it was due to the use of sunscreens.

To avoid the adverse effects of exposure to UV radiation, the correct use of sunscreens and protective clothing should be advocated, taking into consideration the UV index. Currently, however, there is no direct experimental evidence that sunscreens are effective in reducing skin cancer incidence.

Melia et al. concluded that the benefits of education about sun protection are as yet unproven but, if organised effectively, education is likely in the long term to reduce the risk of most skin cancers and photo-aging. They noted that local initiatives require a multidisciplinary approach to ensure co-operation between general practitioners, dermatologists, pathologists and health promotion officers. Such initiatives should be supported by a national programme promoting sun protection and awareness together with national monitoring of changes in knowledge and behaviour.

Integrated coastal management (ICM) plans may help with remedial measures by displaying information in prominent places at the recreational bathing area, developing campaigns and high profile media events. At the local level, ICM has a large role to play in information dissemination.

Physical and Chemical Hazards

Local factors, such as agricultural or, industrial activity, can have a strong influence on the aspects of physical and chemical water quality. Therefore, before standards can be set, it is essential to understand the general characteristics of the water body of interest, together with the effect of local environmental conditions, the processes affecting the concentrations of the physical and chemical variables, and the factors that may modify the toxicity of these variables. It may, therefore, be more appropriate to identify water quality standards on a local basis rather than to adopt national standards for physicochemical aspects of recreational water quality. In determining the likely hazards of physicochemical variables, it is important to evaluate the degree of exposure that recreational users will encounter.

During an inspection for chemical hazards, attention should be paid to the presence of industrial effluent disposal facilities, such as outfalls, sewers and rivers, tributaries, streams or ditches. Adjacent activities and facilities, such as intensive agriculture, electricity generating stations, dredging operations, naval bases, shipyards and terminals, should also be identified and their impact should be assessed.

The assessment should also consider the impact of physical characteristics of the local beach and of the meteorological conditions on the dispersion and dilution of contaminants in the recreational-use area. During an inspection it may be necessary to collect representative water samples to confirm the presence of specific chemical contaminants, to establish their magnitude and variability, to identify the source(s) and to evaluate human exposures and health affects.

Chemical analyses should only be undertaken where standard, replicable and reliable methods are available. In some cases, simple physical tests, such as pH, turbidity or colour, can be measured on-site and used as surrogates for general chemical contamination. Routine monitoring for specific chemicals should only be considered when the inspection indicates a significant hazard to human health.

In assessing local problems, initial screening for risks associated with ingestion may be undertaken by applying the WHO Guidelines for Drinking-Water Quality , with an appropriate correction factor. Although the Guidelines for Drinking-Water Quality are not, generally, based upon short-term exposures, for the purpose of assessing the risk associated with occasional use of recreational waters, public health authorities can use a reference value of 100 times the value Guideline (for other than acute adverse effects) for an initial screening assessment of recreational water pollution with chemicals with known health effects arising from long-term exposure. It should be emphasised that the exceedence of such a reference value does not necessarily imply a risk, but indicate that public health authorities should evaluate the situation.

If, on consideration, it seems probable that contamination is occurring and recreational users are exposed to significant quantities, chemical analysis will be required to support a quantitative risk assessment. Care should be taken in designing the sampling programme to account, for example, for temporal variations and the effects of water currents. If resources are limited and the situation is complex, samples should be taken first at the point considered to give rise to the worst conditions. Only if this gives cause for concern should there be a need for more extensive sampling.

It is important when evaluating physicochemical hazards that the risks are not overestimated, in relation to risks from other hazards, such as drowning or microbiological contamination, which will be almost invariably much greater.

In areas that are used or proposed for bathing, it is suggested that physico-chemical variables such as pH, salinity, aesthetics, clarity, turbidity, colour, oil and grease, inorganic and organic chemicals are considered. Analytical methods and the minimum sample volumes to be taken for these variables are fully detailed in Bartram and Ballance.

8

Sanitation Inspection in Recreational Areas

A sanitary inspection is a search for, and evaluation of, existing and potential microbiological hazards that could affect the safe use of a particular stretch of recreational water or bathing beach. It provides the foundation required to design and implement an effective water quality sampling programme and provides valuable information to assist in the interpretation of water quality data. In particular, it provides public health authorities with information to aid the selection of sampling locations, times and frequencies, in order to estimate more accurately water quality and therefore to allow for sound risk management decisions.

A comprehensive sanitary inspection of an existing recreational area should be conducted annually, just prior to the bathing season. The annual inspection should not only look for new sources of microbiological hazards but also review the adequacy of any sampling programme and corrective measures in place to deal with existing hazards. Further inspections should be conducted along with routine sampling during the bathing season, in order to identify recent events and their impact on water quality. During the peak bathing season additional inspections at different days and times of the day may provide a more complete picture of the bathing area. Comprehensive inspections should be conducted prior to any major new or proposed activity which could significantly alter the microbiological quality of the water in an existing recreational water use area. A sanitary inspection should therefore be carried out as part of, or in response to, any proposal to expand or develop a new recreational bathing area. The findings of the inspection should receive prime consideration in any decision to proceed with development. A comprehensive annual sanitary inspection consists of four steps:

— Pre-inspection preparations.

— An on-site visit.

— The preparation of a preliminary report including recommendations on location of sampling sites and changes to the sampling frequency if necessary.

— The preparation of a final assessment report often in combination with water quality data.

While sampling, important field data can be obtained at each bathing area by inspecting specific sources of pollution. Microbial contamination may be suspected, for example, when inspection reveals abnormal colouration or odour of the water at the bathing site. In the Mediterranean coastal area where the influence of tides is minimal, changes in microbiological quality are mainly due to riverine and direct, especially urban, discharges at the bathing site.

The microbiological contamination produced by long sea outfalls, if well designed, is normally diluted and should not influence the microbiological quality of the bathing area. Land-based sources of contamination are normally associated with smaller discharges or with the likelihood of heavy rain events, characteristic of the Mediterranean climate at the end of the summer period, where a great amount of water falls in a very short period of time. Heavy rain may wash out faeces from pastures or other agricultural land and directly influence microbiological water quality. Studies in other regions also document pulses of poor water quality associated with rainfall events.

In inland recreational waters the main sources of pollution are water inlets. Therefore, influences from rivers, natural watercourses and, particularly around populated areas, combined sewer overflows, produce important changes in the microbiological quality of bathing waters. Sporadic malfunctioning of sewerage systems can produce similar problems.

These events, if recent, can sometimes be recognised visually at the recreational site by changes in the appearance of the water. In marine recreational waters, a field analysis of the salinity can indicate the discharges of freshwater at the bathing site. Such measurements indicate indirectly, that land-borne discharges are occurring.

Pre-inspection Preparations

The collection and review of any existing data or reports on the area, including reports of previous inspections, will allow a thorough and efficient on-site evaluation. Topographical maps and aerial photographs are useful tools for locating activities and features that could affect water quality and for establishing sampling sites. Historical data on tides, currents, prevailing winds, rainfall and discharges of sewage, storm overflows and combined sewer overflows, and urban and agricultural effluents should be collected and reviewed to determine the impact of these events, (either singly or collectively) on water quality.

Depending on the availability of water quality data, experts conducting the annual inspection may need to collect samples for microbiological analyses. Therefore, adequate numbers of sterile sample bottles and sampling equipment should be readily available and prior arrangements should be made with the microbiology laboratory to process samples promptly after collection. Arrangements should be made to meet with user groups and with individuals in charge of any facility or activity that affects, or has the potential to affect, water quality in the recreational area. It will be essential to obtain the trust and co-operation of the groups or individuals if the survey is to provide an accurate assessment of water quality and to identify and remedy unacceptable water quality.

On-site Visit

The purpose of the on-site visit is to identify and evaluate all existing and potential sources of microbiological contamination that could affect the safe use of the area. Attention should be paid to the presence of sewage disposal facilities, including long sea outfalls, industrial outfalls, seabird colonies, sanitary sewers, and rivers, tributaries, streams or ditches receiving sewage, storm water or agricultural runoff. All data recorded should be added to the catalogue of basic characteristics to form a catalogue of inspections that would enable the tracking of trends and influences.

Visual faecal pollution (including sanitary plastics), sewage odour and suspicious water colour should also be considered as an immediate indication of unacceptable water quality. Adjacent industries should also be identified and their impact assessed. The impact of local geography and meteorological conditions on water quality should also be evaluated. In most cases it will be necessary to collect representative water samples to confirm the presence of faecal pollution, to establish its variability and to identify the source. Non-toxic fluorescent tracer dyes, bacteriophages or faecal sterol biomarkers (coprostanol and 24-ethylcoprostanol) may also be helpful to identify sources of contamination.

Epidemiological studies have shown that bathers can be a significant source of pathogenic micro-organisms. In small bathing areas with a lot of bathers and a low rate of water turnover, the person to person disease transmission has to be considered, even if there is no source of faecal pollution from the outside. The assessment may therefore need to consider measures to control microbiological water pollution by bathers in the area. This is especially important in shallow, enclosed areas used by young children where water circulation and flushing rates are low. Intensive studies to locate sources of pollution and to propose remedial actions have been undertaken successfully. A specially designed form can assist in the process of comprehensive sanitary inspection.

Sampling Location and Time

The first step in planning a sampling activity is to define clearly the objective; in most cases the objective will be either exploratory (assessment) or monitoring (surveillance). While the former is designed to provide preliminary or "one-off information about a site, the latter is undertaken for regulatory or non-regulatory purposes". For a recreational water use area, both objectives may initially coincide. Exploratory sampling will be required to define subsequent sampling.

The selection of sampling sites, time and frequency of sample collection should attempt to capture the overall microbiological quality of the water at the recreational water use area. These choices should be based upon the information gathered during the sanitary inspection. The selection of sampling stations and time of sampling should take into consideration, variables known to affect water quality, such as the length of the bathing area, presence and periodicity of point and non-point sources of faecal contamination, influences of local weather, the physical characteristics of the bathing area and the presence of bathers. For example, at bathing areas with no detectable sources of external faecal contamination, samples should be collected at the places with the greatest bather densities.

Bathing areas known to be influenced by direct or indirect faecal contamination will require additional sampling sites to help define the degree and extent of pollution. The time of day can be an important source of variation especially at beaches with significant tides. Consideration should also be given to collecting samples at times when bather densities are greatest for example, afternoons at weekends.

Sampling frequency can also influence the acquisition of reliable information on microbiological pollution in a bathing area. For those laboratories with limited economic or human resources it is better to direct efforts towards increasing sampling frequency instead of confirming presumptive results for Escherichia coli and faecal streptococci. The sampling frequency adopted in many programmes and assessments is fortnightly during the bathing season. Some authors have advocated more frequent samplings such as weekly or more, especially in the peak season in temperate climates and others maintain lower intensity monitoring (e.g. monthly) outside the bathing season.

Evidence suggests that once an understanding of quality behaviour has been developed through relatively intensive monitoring and sanitary surveys, then reduced sampling frequencies may be justifiable and can contribute to reducing the burden of monitoring. For colder climates where the bathing season is restricted by weather, water sampling should be concentrated in that period where historical data show a higher probability of favourable weather conditions for recreational activities. If abnormal favourable weather conditions appear, more frequent sampling should be carried out, especially in freshwater resources with poor water circulation that may be overcrowded under those circumstances.

Monitoring a bathing area or a site to reconfirm repeated failure to meet a guideline or poor water quality has little value. Equally, sampling frequency can be reduced when an area is known, through historical microbiological data, to have consistently good microbiological quality and when it is known from the catalogue of basic characteristics that it will not be subjected to pollution influences because potential sources of contamination are absent. In these situations only occasional confirmatory sampling will be required. Such an approach will direct resources to those beaches known to have variable water quality.

Resampling and new sanitary inspection, following the detection of unexpected peak values, is essential to establish the cause of the observed peak. An exhaustive investigation, including an inspection of the site and possible collection of additional samples to locate the source or sources of pollution, is also essential where the cause is known not to be due to a sporadic event.

Sampling Procedures

Sampling in chest depth water, typically 1.2-1.5 m depth, represents areas of greatest bather density although sampling at ankle depth may be appropriate to determine risk to young children. Microbiological counts from surface samples have been shown to have a tendency to be higher than those beneath the surface, but the epidemiological significance of this has yet to be studied. Therefore samples should be collected from beneath the surface. Precise sampling recommendations vary, for example 30 cm below the surface is indicated by the American Public Health Association (APHA) and the European Community (EC) Directive, while the World Health Organization (WHO) and the United Nations Environment Programme (UNEP) have proposed 25 cm. Every sample within a monitoring programme should be taken as near as possible to the defined sampling location.

Care must be taken to avoid external contamination during sample collection. Sterilised sample bottles should be opened with the opening facing downward and should be held by the base and submerged in the water. At the appropriate depth, the bottle should be turned upwards with the mouth facing the current (if any). After retrieving the bottle, some water should be discarded to leave an air space of at least 2.5 cm to allow mixing by shaking before examination. The utmost care must be taken at all times not to touch the top of the bottle during removal or replacement of the cap.

The sample volume should be sufficient to carry out all the required tests. In practice, 300-500 ml are adequate. If Salmonella, Vibrio cholerae or enteroviruses are to be analysed, as required by some authorities or under certain circumstances, greater volumes of water will be necessary. Bottles of borosilicate glass or suitable autoclavable plastic are recommended. They should have screw caps that withstand repeated sterilisation at 121°C or 180°C. All sampling bottles should be correctly labelled with the reference of the sampling point. Additional information of the time of collection, temperature of water and other observations should be recorded on sample record sheets designed for this purpose.

Sample Storage

There is little published information available that gives a consensus on the time limit for storage of samples to avoid changes in the concentrations of indicator organisms. Storage times should be as short as possible and it is recommended here that samples should be analysed as soon as possible, preferably within 8 hours of collection. If samples cannot be analysed within 24 hours field analysis should be considered. Immediately after collection, the samples should be stored in insulated boxes with cooling packs and/or ice. Samples should be kept in the dark and the temperature of the cooling box maintained below 10°C where possible.

This temperature may be difficult to reach and so in practice samples should be kept as cold as possible, but not frozen. In practical terms these storage conditions can have at best only a limited effect on reducing variations in bacterial populations. It is generally accepted that changes in microbial populations in water samples will begin to occur around 2 hours after collection; within 6 hours the samples are likely to have altered significantly particularly if no cooling mechanism was available and the samples were exposed to light.

The key factor to consider in storage and transport of samples is time between collection and analysis rather than the time between collection and receipt at the laboratory. Ideally, the temperature of the insulated box should be controlled and recorded, as should the storage time. This information should be considered in the interpretation of results. Storage under these conditions should be as short as possible, and samples should be analysed promptly after collection.

Indicator Organisms

Natural waters are subject to important changes in their microbial quality that arise from agricultural use, discharges of sewage or wastewater resulting from human activity or storm water runoff. Sewage effluents contain a wide variety of pathogenic micro-organisms that may pose a health hazard to the human population when the effects are discharged into recreational waters. The density and variety of these pathogens are related to the size of the human population, the seasonal incidence of the illness, and dissemination of pathogens within the community.

Many waterborne pathogens are difficult to detect and/or quantify and the specific methodology to detect them in environmental water samples has still to be developed. While faecal streptococci are suggested as the recommended indicator for salt water, either faecal streptococci or Escherichia coli can be used for monitoring freshwaters. Additional variables can be investigated if they are considered relevant, such as the spores of Clostridium perfringens in tropical waters where the traditional indicators may increase in number in soil and water. Staphylococci are generally assumed to serve as indicators of water pollution deriving from bathers themselves (i.e. by shedding from the body surface). The epidemiological significance of the recovery of Staphylococci remains unclear.

Thermotolerant (faecal) coliforms constitute the subset of total coliforms that possess a more direct and closer relationship with homeothermic faecal pollution. These bacteria conform to all the criteria used to define total coliforms, but in addition they grow and ferment lactose with production of gas and acid at 44.5 ± 0.2°C within the first 48 hours of incubation. For this reason, the term "thermotolerant coliforms" rather than "faecal coliforms" is a more accurate name for this group. The physiological basis of the elevated temperature phenotype in the thermotolerant coliforms has been described as a thermotolerant adaptation of proteins to, and their stability at, the temperatures found in the enteric tracts of animals.

Thermotolerant coliforms include strains of the genera Klebsiella and Escherichia. The thermotolerant coliform definition is not based on strictly taxonomic criteria, but on specific biochemical reactions or on the appearance of characteristic colonies on selective and/or differential culture media. Certain Enterobacter and Citrobacter strains are also able to grow under the conditions defined for thermotolerant coliforms. E. coli is, however, the only biotype of the family Enterobacteriaceae that is almost always faecal in origin. Therefore, the thermotolerant coliform group when used should ideally be replaced by E. coli as an indicator of faecal pollution. For the purpose of water testing, most E. coli can be confirmed by a positive indole test and by their inability to use citrate in the culture medium. Alternatively, E. coli can be distinguished easily enzymatically by the lack of urease or presence of b-glucuronidase enzymes. The enzymes can be recognised easily using culture media that contain specific substrata.

However, several studies have indicated the limitation of both the thermotolerant coliform group and E. coli as ideal faecal indicators or pathogen index organisms. Several thermotolerant Klebsiella strains have been isolated from environmental samples with high levels of carbohydrates in the apparent absence of faecal pollution. Similarly, other members of the thermotolerant coliform group, including E. coli, have been detected in some pristine areas and have been associated with regrowth in drinking water distribution systems. The principal disadvantages of this organism as an indicator in water are: (i) its detection in other environments without faecal contamination, and (ii) its low survival capability in aquatic environments when compared with faecal pathogens.

Faecal streptococci have received widespread acceptance as useful indicators of faecal pollution in natural aquatic ecosystems. These organisms show a close relationship with health hazards associated with bathing in marine and freshwater environments,. They are not as ubiquitous as coliforms, they are always present in the faeces of warm-blooded animals, and it is believed that they do not multiply in sewage-contaminated waters.

The group called faecal streptococci includes species of different sanitary significance and survival characteristics. In addition, the proportion of the species of this group is not the same in animal and human faeces. The taxonomy of this group, comprising species of two genera Enterococcus and Streptococcus, has been subject to extensive revision in recent years

The lack of a strong relationship between faecal indicators and health outcomes in a number of epidemiological studies in warm tropical waters may, in part, relate to the inappropriate nature of E. coli or faecal streptococci as indices of waterborne pathogens in these recreational waters. In this context an alternative index group, sulphite-reducing clostridia or spores of Clostridium perfringens, have been proposed and are used in Hawaii.

It is important to note that spores of C. perfringens do not act as an indicator for non-sewage or animal faecal contamination in general, and therefore they are only suitable as indicator organisms for parasitic protozoa and viruses from sewage-impacted waters. Their resistance to disinfectants may also be an advantage for indexing disinfectant-resistant pathogens. Simple anaerobic culture is possible for C. perfringens spores after a short heat treatment to remove vegetative cells. Confirmation of their presence may be assisted by the addition of a methylumbelliferyl phosphate substrate to the growth medium.

Other indicator organisms for sewage, but also specific for human sewage are the bacteriophages to Bacteroides fragilis HSP40. These B. fragilis phages appear to survive in a manner that is similar to the hardier human enteric viruses under a range of conditions. Their numbers in sewage such as the F-specific RNA bacteriophages may be an order of magnitude lower than various coliphages. Furthermore, only 1-5 per cent of humans may excrete these phages, and thus they may be unsuitable pathogen indicator organisms for small communities.

Analytical Methods

Most Probable Number (MPN)

Most Probable Number (MPN) analysis is a statistical method based on the random dispersion (Poisson) of micro-organisms per volume in a given sample. Classically, this assay has been performed as a multiple-tube fermentation test. Although the technique is rather time consuming (taking between five and seven days), several laboratories prefer it to other methods of water analysis because it is applicable to all sample types.

The MPN technique is generally conducted in three sequential phases (presumptive, confirmatory, and complete), each phase requiring 1 to 2 days of incubation. In the initial or presumptive phase, three volumes of samples (usually 10, 1, and 0.1 ml) are inoculated into 3, 5, or 10 tubes containing the appropriate medium to allow the target bacteria to grow. In this test, it is assumed that any single viable target organism in the sample will result in growth or a positive reaction in the medium.

After the incubation period, all the inoculated presumptive positive tubes must be inoculated into a more selective medium to confirm the presence of the target bacteria. The confirmation test is reliable evidence, but not proof, that the target bacteria have been detected. Therefore, subsamples of the confirmed positive reactions should be inoculated onto a selective agar medium and several verification tests should be carried out. This completed test is generally conducted on 10 per cent of the positive tubes as a quality control measure. For practical purposes, the number of positive and negative tubes in the confirmatory phase of the technique is generally used to determine the MPN of the target bacteria by using tables of positive and negative tube reactions.

Membrane Filtration

The membrane filtration (MF) technique is based on the entrapment of the bacterial cells by a membrane filter. After the water is filtered, the membrane is placed on an appropriate medium and incubated. Discrete colonies with typical appearance are counted after 24-48 hours, and the population density of the target bacteria, usually described as cfu per 100 ml in the original sample, can be calculated from the filtered volumes and dilutions used. This technique is more precise than the MPN technique, but the MF test can only be used for low-turbidity waters with low concentrations of background micro-organisms.

Data Recording

Analysis may be performed as part of a regulatory monitoring programme, as part of a survey of an area used for water recreation, or as part of an epidemiological study in which water quality is related to risks to health from infectious diseases. Each approach has its own requirements which are specified at the outset by the regulatory authority or the study director. One of the most important functions of the analyst is to provide reliable and accurate results in a form that can be recorded for statistical interpretation and reporting.

An individual record must be produced for each site inspection or sample and should include the location and reference of the sampling site (that should ideally be equal to the code number of the sample), the date, the time, weather conditions, tide, water temperature, results of visual inspection for abnormal conditions, sources of contamination and the name of the inspector or sampler. Sampling records should also list the laboratory procedures and results (method of analysis, dilutions or volumes analysed, time of analysis, results for each step, any anomalies in the analysis of results and the name of the analyst). Ideally, record forms should occupy a single page.

Forms should be conveniently archived, because they will be used later by the data handlers for transcription to the database and they will be analysed for the purposes of preparing the report of the monitoring or survey programme. Great care should be taken in preparing the report and its contents and format should be agreed by those responsible for analysis, data handling and for reporting results and, if necessary, by those responsible for co-ordinating results of regional, national and international programmes. For quality assurance, it should be possible to conduct an "audit trail" through the whole process of visiting the site, analysing the sample and filing the results on the database.

The results of microbiological analyses of water quality must always be regarded as an estimate of the water quality at the time and site of sampling, rather than as an absolute determination. All enumeration methods depend on the assumption that bacteria and other micro-organisms are randomly distributed in water samples and that the samples conform to the Poisson distribution.

In reality, the clumping of bacteria and their aggregation on particles cause samples to depart from the Poisson distribution, thereby introducing additional error. There is little that can be done to reduce this error, apart from taking representative samples (free of sediment and other solid matter) and mixing the contents of the sampling bottles vigorously before taking sub-samples for analysis. It has been shown that two halves of the same sample can vary widely in the counts observed.

A historical record of water quality in a bathing area, in normal and extreme situations, enables the selection of the most appropriate dilutions and facilitates the correct enumeration of the final density of indicator organisms that has to be reported as the total number of cfu per 100 ml.

Great care should go into the counting and recording of analytical results in order to avoid recording results wrongly, leading to errors that can result in statistical misinterpretations of water quality at the recreational area. Typical sources of error in the laboratory are caused by operator fatigue and mistakes, such as mislabelling of bottles, Petri dishes and tubes, and errors in preparing and transferring volumes and dilutions of samples. Because labels attached to the lids of Petri dishes, tubes and bottles can be transposed, the labels should be placed on the dish, tube or bottle itself, because these contain the culture medium. Although it may not be obvious, operators vary in the accuracy with which they count colonies and, in addition, unsuspected partial colour blindness can interfere with the interpretation of biochemical reactions of target colonies or in tubes of diagnostic media. Mistakes and errors can be minimised by proper training and supervision of samplers and analysts in their duties. In addition, laboratory quality controls and the careful application of standard procedures for analysis are essential. Standard procedures should be written correctly and copies should always be available for reference in the laboratory.

Interpretation and Reporting

Interpretation of results and reporting do not normally involve the analyst. Nevertheless, strict adherence to analytical control procedures make it possible for queries about unusual or anomalous results to be referred back to the analyst and sampler, through an audit trail. Although the absolute values may differ with different approaches described, there is a high level of agreement on the water microbiological quality qualification of the beach in relation to compliance.

One of the features of microbiological studies of water quality at recreational areas is the wide variations in results, temporally and spatially that are much greater than those caused by laboratory procedures. With effective quality control in the laboratory, variability caused by procedures, such as sub-sampling from the same bottle or by the enumeration procedures themselves, are little greater than expected from the assumption of random distribution of bacteria in the sample and of the Poisson theory, particularly when the mean number is low.

A single limit standard leads to water of borderline quality and with low variability, consistently passing, whereas water which is usually of high quality, but is occasionally affected by intermittent pollution, would fail, even though the former arguably poses a greater risk to health. More detailed study of the results in the latter case might identify the causes of failure and enable advice to be given to the public not to use the water when poor conditions are expected, or enable remedial action to be taken.

One way of identifying systematic changes in water quality, or of pinpointing sudden deterioration of water quality at a recreational area, is to create control charts. Water quality data points are plotted sequentially, as they are obtained, against time on a chart. Any existing historical data from specific bathing areas can be used to create control charts and helps to identify patterns of behaviour.

Once the investigation or monitoring programme is completed, the information is assembled into a comprehensive report. The main body of the report should state the objectives; the manner in which the programme was conducted, with a full description of the recreational area; a historical account of problems and developments; the strategy and reports of inspection, sampling and analysis; significant results obtained; a discussion of the results; and conclusions and recommendations for action.

Many of the readers will not have a technical background and therefore an easily readable and accurate "executive summary" should be provided at the front of the report. This gives such readers the main points of the report and invites them to follow-up areas of interest. The report itself should enable the technical reader to understand fully the way in which the study was carried out.

Larger bodies of data should be placed in an appendix, so as not to interrupt the flow of the report. A typical report of a sanitary inspection and microbiological analysis includes the following: a description of the survey area(s) and sampling stations, and of any identified hazard(s) and source(s) of pollution (photographs and maps would be useful); the results of the study, including those of the sanitary inspections and microbiological analysis; an in-depth assessment of the risks associated with identified hazards and/or poor water quality; recommendations about the suitability of the area for recreational water use; description and evaluation of various options for improving conditions and thereby for reducing aesthetic and health hazards to users; and recommendations for action, including modifications if necessary, to the monitoring programmes.

The results and recommendations should be discussed with any interested parties before the report is released formally. A contingency plan should also be developed, with the assistance of any interested parties, to investigate and respond to cases of illness or to any unforeseen event or condition that could lead to a deterioration in water quality and possibly increase the risk of illness or danger to bathers. Consideration should also be given to preparing a nontechnical report for the general public.

All laboratories should guarantee that the results of the microbiological analysis of a water sample actually originated from the sample and were not introduced accidentally during sampling or analysis. To support this guarantee, internal and external quality controls should be implemented.

It is sufficient to note here that the quality of recreational water is of great public concern and is often used in publicity to attract visitors to recreational areas. Several countries have developed regular information services, using television, teletext, newspapers and radio to supplement bulletins in municipal buildings and on public notice boards at the recreational areas. Generally, the public simply want to know if it is safe to use the water and most people have little understanding of the meaning of bacterial counts, let alone their variability. The information presented to the public, therefore, should be direct and unequivocal, up-to-date and not open to misinterpretation.

9

Quality Assurance

Quality assurance is a management method that is defined as all those planned and systematic actions needed to provide adequate confidence that a product, service or result will satisfy given requirements for quality and be fit for use. A quality assurance programme is defined as the sum total of the activities aimed at achieving that required standard.

Quality assurance for a recreational water monitoring programme will, apart from helping to ensure that the results obtained are correct, increase the confidence of funding bodies and the public. Quality Assurance extends to all aspects of data collection from sanitary surveys to laboratory procedures. Unless the data can be checked they should not be included in any assessment; unconfirmed observations have little value and can result in misclassification.

The components of a QA programme are often grouped into three levels, variously labelled: the strategic or organisational level ; the tactical or functional level (dealing with general practices such as training, facilities, operation of QA); and the operational level (dealing with the Standard Operating Procedures (SOPs) worksheets and other aspects of day to day operations).

There is no single method for establishing a QA system. Each organisation has its own problems that will require special consideration and planning. However, once the decision to implement a QA system has been taken and the necessary funds and facilities have been made available, then a plan must be drawn up. For a new project the QA system can be drawn up before the start but if the project is already established then a QA system can be retrofitted. In the latter situation, existing practices must be evaluated with respect to QA needs and any QA checks and procedures that are already in place. It is better to build on procedures already in place and only to remove them if they are clearly unsatisfactory. If too many changes are imposed too quickly, especially where they are seen to increase work load, they are unlikely to be met with a favourable response and implementation will be poor. The QA programme must be seen to be practical and realistic and not to include trivial or unnecessarily time-consuming or difficult tasks.

Quality Manual

The Quality Manual is composed of the management documents needed to implement the QA programme and includes:

— A quality policy statement, including objectives and commitments.

— The organisation and management structure of the project, its place in any parent organisation and relevant organisational charts.

— The relationship between management, technical operations, support services and the quality system.

— Procedures for control and maintenance of documentation.

— Job descriptions for key staff and reference to the job descriptions of other staff.

— Identification of approved signatories.

— Procedures for ensuring traceability of all paperwork, data and reports.

— The laboratory's scope for calibrations and tests.

— Arrangements for ensuring that all new projects are reviewed to ensure that there are adequate resources to manage them properly.

— Reference to the calibration, verification and testing procedures used.

— Procedures for handling calibration and test items.

— Reference to the major equipment and reference measurement standards used.

— Reference to procedures for calibration, verification and maintenance of equipment.

— Reference to verification practices including inter-laboratory comparisons, proficiency testing programmes, use of reference materials and internal quality control schemes.

— Procedures to be followed for feedback and corrective actions whenever testing discrepancies or departure from documented procedures are detected.

— Procedures to be followed for feedback and corrective actions whenever testing discrepancies or departure from documented procedures are detected.

— Complaints procedure.

— Procedures for protecting confidentiality and property rights.

— Procedures for audit and review.

Training

The development of the programme must include all staff. Typically, the management commit resources, establish policy and standards, approve plans, assign responsibilities and maintain accountability. The supervisory staff take responsibility for the development and implementation of the programme and operating personnel provide technical expertise and advice. At all stages, the operating personnel must be consulted about the practicalities of any proposed changes. In turn, they must notify management of any problems or changes that may affect the programme.

Standard Operating Procedures

Standard Operating Procedures (SOPs) are the documents detailing all specific operations and methods, including sampling, transportation, analysis, use of and calibration of equipment, production of reports and interpretation of data. They are the internal reference manual for the particular procedure and should detail every relevant step. Anybody of the appropriate training level should be able to follow the SOP. They should, where necessary, cross-reference other SOPs and refer to them by number.

Method SOPs may originate from organisations such as the International Organization for Standardization (ISO), British Standards Institute (BSI), American Standard Technical Method (ASTM) or from the instructions that come with the test kit where a commercially produced method is used. Such SOPs have the advantage of not requiring verification and save time in writing "in-house" SOPs. However, if they are used they must be used without modification. If any modification at all takes place, the alterations must be documented. Sometimes "in house" methods are preferred, and it is vital that such methods are properly verified. This may be done by reference to scientific literature and by "in house" validation.

The procedure should be written in short, clear sentences. Equipment SOPs should include methods and frequency of maintenance, cleaning, calibration and servicing. Method SOPs should include all the information necessary to carry out the procedure without reference to other documents with the exception of fully documented SOPs.

Any statements regarding ranges for measurement variables such as temperature, weights, etc. should be within the scope of the facility, i.e. not so wide that they affect the result but not so narrow that they are not practically achievable or necessary. Calculations should include any equations and demonstration of statistical control. Where applicable, criteria for the acceptance of data should be stated and acceptable ranges quoted. Disposal methods for reagents, test materials and other consumables should also be stated.

Some SOPs, such as those for office procedures, will be customised. The person most technically competent to carry out the procedure described should write the SOP. An SOP should have a descriptive title and also have a unique reference and version number. The purpose of the SOP should be stated alongside the variables measured, the expected range of values, the limitations of the method and the expected precision and accuracy.

Any documents regarding the source of the method should be stated. Safety notes should include any foreseeable risks involved in the procedure, alongside procedures to minimise risk and procedures in case of an accident. Any special training required for the operator, and special apparatus required for the procedure (including all reagents and materials required) should be stated along with such information as the grade, reference number, size and company of origin. The storage, handling, recording and subsequent disposal of the sample should also be covered in the SOP, including storage temperatures, sample splitting, traceability, and any other issues. The style and format of the final data report should be given where applicable and reporting procedures and archiving requirements should also be included.

Quality Assurance Manager

For larger projects, proper management of QA will require the appointment of a QA manager to liaise with staff, to manage data archives, to conduct regular audits and reviews and to report on any QA issues. The manager is responsible for inspecting all aspects of the system regularly to ensure compliance, for reporting on such inspections and audits to management and for recommending improvements. These activities involve inspecting facilities and procedures regularly, tracing samples and documents back through the system and ensuring that all appropriate records have been kept.

Auditing and Checking Compliance

When all the documentation for the QA system is in place, it should be piloted. During this time, the QA manager should conduct a series of audits covering all aspects of the system. Traceability of data is a key component which can be checked by picking data at random and tracing them back through all relevant paperwork to the sampling procedure. A review of the system with positive and negative areas clearly defined should be written at the end of the pilot phase.

One method of implementation is to apply for accreditation from a recognised QA system. The ISO standard, ISO 9000, is suitable for the monitoring programme as a whole and is available in many countries. These systems are expensive but do allow the QA programme to be assessed independently against an agreed standard. Sometimes formal accreditation is required by regulatory and commercial bodies.

Maintaining Quality Assurance

In order to maintain the QA system, it is necessary to check periodically each area of the system for compliance. This involves auditing the component parts to assess whether they continue to meet the original criteria. This procedure should be formerly documented. Reports on all audits should be made available to management and to the persons responsible for the work concerned. Deviations from required standards must be corrected as soon as possible. The audit must be independent, and should be thorough and unannounced.

Equipment Maintenance

All equipment, whether site, office or laboratory, must be maintained on a regular basis as documented in the relevant SOPs, codes of practice and manufacturer's guidelines. Laboratories must apply standards within the limits established for the care of a particular piece of equipment. This applies to general equipment, such as glassware, as well as to sophisticated analytical instruments and vehicles. It especially applies to field equipment.

The care and cleaning of equipment is very important to ensure analytical quality. Regular internal and external calibration checks must be performed on equipment such as balances, pipettes and pH meters. The frequency of these checks depends on the stability of the equipment in question but should be based on established practice. The form and frequency of these checks should be documented in the relevant SOPs. Calibration and maintenance records should be kept for all equipment, thus allowing the repair status to be monitored.

Sampling

Any analysis can only be as good as the sample taken. Variations in sampling procedures can have a marked effect on the results of analysis. It is very difficult to quantify these effects and therefore procedures for sampling operations should be documented carefully so that all relevant information is recorded at the time of sampling by the field worker.

For any sampling programme, a sampling plan must be prepared to allow full control of the sampling process so that any change seen between two sampling rounds can be attributed to changes in environmental conditions and not to changes in procedure. Items to be considered in preparing a sampling plan include planning issues, fieldwork procedures and field safety issues.

Planning issues include identification of the objective of sampling (e.g. to test compliance with a bathing water regulation), choice of site (location, type of water body), the type and number of samples to be collected (sample types, e.g. water, sediment, the number of samples, appropriate equipment) and timing of sampling (considering the state of tides).

Consideration must be given to sampling SOPs (for equipment, sampling method, storage, etc.), as well as size of sample and sample containers. Preservation must be decided in consultation with staff from the analysing laboratory, who will advise clients on the volume and type of sample and who will usually provide sampling containers and preservatives where necessary. Ensuring field quality control includes the use of blanks, duplicate samples, replicate samples and spiked samples. Storage and holding time must also be considered.

The laboratory staff must be made aware when samples are due to arrive so that they can make the appropriate arrangements. When choosing an analytical laboratory it is important to be aware of the location of the laboratory in relation to the sampling site, as well as the latest time of day that they are prepared to accept samples.

Other factors include deciding where to carry out analysis, i.e. in the laboratory or on site. Some analyses may be better performed on site, such as dissolved oxygen measurements, calibration of field measuring equipment, flow pumps and thermometers, etc. and sample treatments such as filtration. Some samples need to be split or subsampled. Where this is done, great care needs to be taken because samples are frequently very variable.

Contingency plans need to be prepared for situations such as bad weather and vehicle breakdown. Field sampling sheets also need to be prepared. These can be filled in manually on paper forms or on a portable computer providing that the software has been properly validated. When designing field report forms it is important that the place, time and date of sampling, sampling conditions, any field measured variables, equipment used, any necessary sample preparation and the name of the operator are included in the form. Practical difficulties, such as how many samples the field worker will need to carry, parking and access to the site also need to be considered.

Field safety can have a bearing on the quality of data generated where field operators may be inclined to use a less than optimum procedure in order to protect themselves. This must be taken into account when writing the sampling procedure. For example, insisting on sampling water at chest height may deter some operators if the conditions in the water to be sampled are rough. Sampling from boats can be especially hazardous in rough weather.

Even the 30 cm depth stipulation of the European Union's Bathing Water Directive can be difficult to comply with. When devising a plan, areas of risk may have to be borne in mind, including water depth and sampling conditions, currents, wildlife, traffic and weather. Staff must always be provided with the appropriate protective equipment and SOPs should be developed with the safety of operators of paramount concern.

In spite of the difficulties involved in site work, QA is critical at this point. If a good, practical, field QA programme is put into operation, confidence in the data collected should be ensured. All equipment must be kept clean and in good order, and records should be kept of all maintenance and of any irregularities that may affect the results. Conditions in the working area should not expose the operator to undue risk of any type.

Standardised and approved methodologies must be used at all times. If a method proves unworkable on site, then an alternative must be found quickly and agreed by all those involved. Operators must not change procedures without referral to the management procedure. Where unavoidable changes are made, for example, in bad weather, they must be fully documented. Nevertheless, a good sampling plan should make provisions for bad weather.

Prevention of Sample Contamination

It is important that samples are protected from contamination and deterioration before their arrival in the laboratory. This can be ensured by using only recommended sample containers. Where reusable containers are used, it is essential that they have been cleaned properly and, if necessary, sterilised before use. Containers that have been sterilised must remain sterile until the sample is collected.

The inner portion of the sample container should not be touched by the operator. If the seal on the bottle is broken (in the case of a commercially purchased microbiological sample bottle), or if the protective paper or foil has been lost from the top (home-made sampling containers), the bottle should be discarded.

Recommended preservation methods must be used. Where this involves chemical preservatives, the chemicals must be of analytical grade, and provided and tested for efficacy by the analytical laboratory.

Field measurements, such as pH and temperature, must be made on a separate subsample which is then discarded in order not to contaminate samples for interlaboratory analysis. Conductivity measurements should not be made with a sample that has been used previously for measuring pH, because potassium chloride from the pH probe may affect the conductivity reading.

All sample containers should be kept in a clean environment, away from dust, dirt and fumes. Petroleum products and fumes may contaminate samples with heavy metals and hydrocarbons. This can be a major problem on boats, where leaks and seepage of petroleum products are common. Samples must be stored in a cool box or portable refrigerator and transported to the laboratory as soon as possible. Cool boxes are more efficient if they contain some water.

Quality Control (QC) is an essential part of the field QA programme. It requires the collection of replicate samples to check the repeatability of sampling, and the submission of field blanks and duplicates to check for contamination, handling and storage problems and other errors that may affect the results from the time of sampling to the time of analysis. The timing and frequency of these samples should be documented in the sampling plan.

Laboratory Facilities

Except for any on-site analysis, analysis is usually performed in a laboratory. It is essential that any facilities are adequately equipped to deal with the analyses required and are convenient for the delivery of samples. This should have been ascertained before the start of the monitoring programme.

Small-scale organisations responsible for monitoring may find it more convenient to use outside facilities for analysis and sometimes for sampling. In these cases, the use of a laboratory belonging to an accreditation scheme is advisable and, moreover the laboratory should be inspected for compliance by an experienced member of the monitoring programme. An inspection should take into account the following features:

— Lines of communication between staff and management.

— Staff training and qualifications.

— Resources.

— Equipment maintenance and calibration.

— Standard Operating Procedures.

— Traceability of results.

— Sample handling and storage.

Where in-house facilities are used, it is essential that the monitoring work does not overload the laboratory.

Resources (staff, space, equipment and supplies) must be sufficient for the planned workload. The laboratory must be well managed and must conform to all relevant health and safety guidelines. All analyses performed must be within the remit and expertise of the facility and SOPs must be in operation for all analyses.

Procedures for sample handling, transport and storage prior to analysis should ensure that the quality of the sample is not compromised. The condition of each sample and its storage location should be recorded along with its proposed analyses. If the sample is split, this must also be recorded. All samples must be identified uniquely with a number or code. It is important to ensure that the passage of a sample, and any associated paperwork, through the laboratory is fully documented and, therefore, traceable.

Reporting

The efforts of QA are directed ultimately towards ensuring that any data produced are suitable for their intended use; this applies to the results and any interpretations. The first stage in the reporting process is the examination of the results to see if they are fit to report (although raw data should have been checked prior to this stage). Results must be reported accurately and in a way that aids interpretation. To facilitate this, information may need to be included that has a bearing on interpretation, such as sampling conditions or the method of analysis.

All data included must be checked by an experienced analyst with reference to site reports, calibration and QC data. Many laboratories have a system which requires the checking and countersigning of analytical reports (usually by the laboratory manager) to act as a safeguard against erroneous or misleading data leaving the laboratory. This type of system is only effective when conscientiously applied.

Analytical Quality Control

Analytical Quality Control consists of two elements: internal quality control (IQC) and external quality control (EQC). External quality control or inter-laboratory control is carried out periodically and checked by the laboratory responsible for the monitoring system. Internal quality control consists of the operational techniques used by the laboratory staff for continuous assessment of the quality of the results of individual analytical procedures.

The focus is principally on monitoring precision, although accuracy is not ignored. It is necessarily part of the wider QA programme, but differs from it by the emphasis placed on quantifying precision and accuracy. Whereas QA strives to achieve quality by regulating procedures using management techniques, IQC focuses on the individual method and tests its performance against mathematically-derived quality criteria.

Internal Quality Control in Chemical Laboratory

Internal quality control within the chemical laboratory comprises a variety of activities, some of which are described below.

Choice of analytical method: A variety of different analytical methods are usually available for determining the concentration of any variable in a water sample. The choice of method is critical for ensuring that the results of the analysis meet the laboratory's requirements, because different methods have different precisions and sensitivities and are subject to different potential interferences. Consideration must be given to these parameters before a method is chosen. A number of standard methods are available for most of the analytical determinations involved in water quality monitoring, and in some cases the method is named in the regulations. These standard methods frequently include extensive validation data that allow the method to be evaluated easily. In addition, many methods are sanctioned by appropriate international or national organisations. It is important that any method selected meets the individual programme requirements. The performance of a method can be affected unpredictably by many factors.

Before any analytical method is put into routine use it is essential that it is properly validated. A minimum programme of validation includes a number of elements. One of these elements is the determination of linearity - the calibration point should be determined and if possible a linear response curve should be demonstrated. In addition, the limit of detection (the lowest concentration of the variable that can be distinguished from zero with 95 per cent confidence) should be determined. Within-and between-day coefficients of variation should be performed at three concentration levels to determine precision. Analysis of reference materials with known concentrations of the variable, or comparison analysis with existing methods in other laboratories, should be performed where possible.

Validity checking: After a method has been validated, found to be suitable and introduced into routine use in the laboratory, it is necessary to ensure that it continues to produce satisfactory results. Validity checks should be made on every batch of samples, or at frequent, regular intervals if batches are large or if testing is continuous. Validity checking is an extension of the checks carried out before the method was selected and is intended to confirm regularly the conclusions reached at that time.

Calibration check: If a calibration curve is being used, standard solutions should be analysed from time to time within the required range of concentration. The ideal calibration curve is linear within its most useful range, with a regression coefficient of 0.99 or greater. The response of the measuring equipment to the concentration of the variable in a standard solution (in terms of absorbance or some other parameter) should be recorded when it is expected that this parameter will be comparable from assay to assay. In addition, the deviation of individual calibration points from the line of best fit can be used to assess the precision of the calibration, which should be within the mean precision limits for the method.

Use of blanks: Method blanks and, where possible, field blanks should be analysed with each batch of samples. A method blank consists of reagent water, usually double-distilled water. A field blank is reagent water that has been bottled in the laboratory, shipped with sample bottles to the sampling site, processed and preserved as a routine sample and returned with the routine samples to the laboratory for analysis. The analysis of a blank should not yield a value higher than that allowed by the acceptance criteria. This procedure checks interference and the limit of detection of the assay.

Recovery checking: A specimen spiked with a known amount of the variable should be tested in each batch and the closeness of fit to the expected value calculated. In most cases this procedure provides a check on accuracy but, in assays where a variable is extracted from the original matrix (such as in many sample cleanup procedures used prior to chromatographic analysis), it can be used to monitor the extraction step. It is important that the matrix of the spiked specimen matches the real sample matrix as closely as possible. Many laboratories use real samples with low natural values of the variable for this purpose, spiking them with known amounts of the variable and including both the spiked and natural samples in the same assay batch.

Precision and accuracy checks: Precision and accuracy checks are an extension of the validity checking described above. These checks allow the quality of the assay to be monitored over time using techniques such as control charting. The validity checks described above only allow acceptance or rejection of the assay data. Precision and accuracy checking should allow slow deterioration of data quality to be identified and corrected before data have to be rejected. This results in increased efficiency and reduced costs for the laboratory.

Control by duplicate analysis: Use of duplicate analysis as a method of precision checking has two distinct advantages: quality control materials are matrix-matched and the materials are readily available at no extra cost. Because the samples are analysed using the same method, equipment and reagents, the same bias will affect all results. Consequently, duplicate analyses are only useful for checking precision; they provide no indication of the accuracy of the analyses.

Precision control using pooled reference material: A more sophisticated approach is to use acceptance criteria based on warning and action limits. This method has the advantage of providing some monitoring of accuracy but is a viable control only if the material to be used will be stable in storage for sufficient time.

The reference material is normally prepared by taking previously analysed samples with known concentrations of the variable under investigation, mixing them and aliquoting the resultant pool. The aliquots are then stored in readiness for analysis. A small sample of the aliquots is analysed to determine the mean concentration of the variable, and the standard deviation and the coefficient of variance at that concentration level.

Data may be used only if they come from analysis that are in control. This approach requires that the new pool materials must be prepared before the old ones are finished.

A typical precision control exercise would involve the analysis of four aliquots from each pool in each of five assays, thus obtaining 20 results. The material from the pool should be analysed at several different times with different batches, because between batch variance is always slightly greater than within batch variance. Once 20 or more analyses have been made on this pool of material, the mean and standard deviations of the results are calculated. Any result that is more than three standard deviations from the mean is discarded and both of the statistics are recalculated. The mean is the "target" value and ideally, will be a close approximation of the true concentration of the variable in the reference material. The mean and standard deviation become the basis of the acceptance criteria for the assay method and may be used to draw up control charts.

At least three separate reference materials with different mean values of variable concentration should be in use at any one time in order to provide control of the analytical method across a range of concentrations. If precision is checked at only one concentration of the variable, it is impossible to detect whether precision is deteriorating at other concentrations. Use of several reference materials also allows their preparation to be staggered so that they become exhausted at different times. This assures greater continuity of control, because two or more old pools will still be in use during the first few assays of a new reference material.

Although the monitoring of accuracy by assessing deviation from the reference material mean (target value) is possible, care must be taken because the target value is only an approximation of the true value. As reference materials become exhausted and new ones are made, there will be a slow deterioration in accuracy. Accuracy can be safeguarded by regular participation in EQC exercises and by the use of certified reference materials.

Certified reference materials: Certified reference materials (CRMs) are matrix- matched materials with assigned target values and ranges for each variable, reliably determined from data produced by repeated analysis. Target and range values may be generated from data produced by several laboratories using different analytical methods or calculated from data obtained by the use of one analytical method (usually a reference method).

Consequently, there may be bias in the target value. The target values assigned to each variable in the matrix in certified reference materials are generally very close to the true value. For some variables, however, there is an appreciable difference in bias between different analytical methods and this may lead to wide assigned ranges. When a laboratory is not using one of the reference methods the "all method" range may be so wide that it is practically meaningless. Certified reference materials are also only practical for variables that are stable in long-term storage.

Certified reference materials are prepared and checked under carefully controlled conditions and, as a result, they are costly to produce, correspondingly expensive to purchase and they may be difficult to obtain in some countries. Some authorities advocate the routine use of CRMs as precision control materials, but it is more cost effective to use them for the periodic checking of accuracy, in combination with a rigorous IQC programme.

Use of control charts: The principle of control charts is that IQC data can be graphically plotted so that they can be readily used and interpreted. Consequently, a control chart must be easy to use, easy to understand and easy to act upon. The Shewhart chart is the most widely used control chart. It is a graph with time (or assay batch) on the x-axis and the concentration of the variable in the reference material on the y-axis. Target, warning and action lines are marked parallel to the x-axis.

Data obtained from precision control using reference materials (as described above) are usually plotted on a Shewhart chart. In this application, the target line is at the mean concentration of the variable for that specific pool of material and warning lines are placed at two standard deviations to either side of the target line. Provided the distribution is normal, 95 per cent of results from assays in control will fall between the two warning lines. Action lines are normally placed at three standard deviations to either side of the target line and 99 per cent of normally distributed results should be between the action lines.

In the regular use of a Shewhart chart, an aliquot from an appropriate reference material is analysed with every batch of samples and the measured concentration of the variable in the aliquot is plotted on the chart. Normally, no more than 1 in 20 consecutive results should fall outside the warning lines. If this frequency is exceeded, or if a result falls outside the action lines, the method is out of control.

The scatter of the assay results for the reference material around the target line provides an indication of the precision of the method, while the mean of the assay results relative to the target value indicates whether there is any bias (consistent deviation) in the results. If the analysis on one or more of the control specimens yields a result that it is outside the warning or action lines on the chart, the following action should be taken:

— A single result outside the warning lines should lead to careful review of data from that analytical batch and two or three subsequent batches.

— Results outside the warning lines more frequently than once every 20 consecutive analyses of control specimens should prompt detailed checking of the analytical method and rejection of the assay data.

— A result outside the action limits should prompt detailed checking of the analytical method and rejection of the assay data.

Internal Quality Control in Microbiology Laboratory

Internal quality control in microbiology laboratories poses special problems of reproducibility due to the naturally wide variation in the number of organisms found between subsamples. Apart from method and field blanks (where the method blank should be sterile distilled water and the field blank should be a natural sample either guaranteed free of the test organisms or sterilised natural water), control samples should be analysed which are known to contain appropriate numbers of the micro-organisms that are normally sought. It is possible to purchase sets of freeze dried wild-type bacterial reference cultures for quality control and accreditation requirements. These cultures should be reconstituted and diluted with quarter strength Ringer's solution to give a suitable number of organisms similar to that which would normally be seen in the natural samples. These cultures are expensive and therefore it is not feasible to use a new culture for every batch of samples or media.

However, frequent subculture of reference strains is to be discouraged due to problems with contamination and mutation. This is a special problem with coliphage analysis, where mutation of the host species can prevent the detection of viral plaques. This problem can be solved by freezing down the cultures in glycerol broth and either storing in liquid nitrogen or a -70 °C freezer or, more conveniently, on commercially available plastic storage beads and freezing at -20 °C. Alternatively, some media companies supply standardised cultures in an easy to use form. These cultures may be qualitative or quantitative and have the advantage of eliminating the trial and error diluting of suspensions to achieve the desired count.

Shewhart charts can be used in water microbiology despite the problems of natural random variation. However, this means that wide control limits are necessary. The microbiology laboratory should carry out several duplicate analyses regularly and plot the results on a control chart. Each half should be treated as a separate sample and analysed routinely. They should be inserted in the sample run in a random fashion without the knowledge of the analyst and all results should be read by the same person. The first count should be recorded on the control sheet, and the corresponding CI for the second count entered. The second count is then recorded along these figures. If this count falls outside the CI, this fact should be highlighted. If a Shewhart chart is made up of these results, then any trend can be identified. If, over a period of time, the second count falls outside the CI for more than 95 per cent of the time, the reason should be investigated. As with the use of duplicate samples in chemistry, this approach keeps a check on precision and not on accuracy.

In addition to blanks and a manufactured control, the use of a known wild positive can be included. This can be chosen from the last batch of samples run. However, there can be problems with this, due to alteration in bacterial numbers over time and storage.

All prepared media should be checked for performance and sterility and identified by batch reference number. Both negative and positive control strains of bacteria should be included. Manufacturers of dried media will usually recommend control strains if requested. Where a medium is meant to inhibit the growth of a particular organism, this should also be tested.

External Quality Control

External quality control is a way of establishing the accuracy of analytical methods and procedures by comparing the results of analyses made in one laboratory with the results obtained by others conducting the same analysis on the same material. This is usually accomplished by one laboratory sending out sets of samples, with known and unknown concentrations of variables, to all of the specified laboratories. Each participant analyses the samples for the specified variables and reports the results to the reference laboratory.

The results from all participating laboratories are collated by the organisers of the EQC programme and then subjected to detailed statistical analysis. A report to each laboratory is generated, giving a target value for the reference sample or samples (usually consensus mean or median), a histogram illustrating distribution of results for each material, and an individual performance score relating the individual laboratory results to the target value. The calculations for performance indicators are often quite complex because multiple specimens have to be considered and the method variance varies with the concentration of the variable. However, the general principle of providing a method of performance comparison remains the same in all EQC exercises.

External quality control reports should indicate clearly whether performance is satisfactory or not. If it is not satisfactory, two general actions must be taken. First, the analysis at fault must be examined to determine the cause of poor performance. Secondly, the IQC programme that allowed the deterioration to progress unchecked must be closely examined to establish where inadequacies exist. Both must be corrected.

The general objective of EQC is to assess the accuracy of analytical results measured in participating laboratories and to improve interlaboratory comparability. Wherever possible, laboratories should participate in EQC programmes for each variable that is analysed routinely. This is only worthwhile where IQC is also part of a laboratory's normal procedures. Participation in relevant EQC programmes, and maintenance of adequate performance in those programmes, is often a requirement for laboratory accreditation.

The organisation of an EQC exercise is expensive. Large quantities of stable reference materials must be prepared, these materials must be transported to the participating laboratories, data must be analysed and detailed reports on performance must be prepared. Participating laboratories are usually charged for the service provided.

10

Resources and Implementation

Monitoring programmes, by necessity, must be commensurate with the socio-economic and technical and scientific development of the country where they are implemented. For example the extent of development of national legislation and co-ordinating or oversight programmes will affect activities undertaken. Similarly, more complex analytical variables require highly trained technicians and costly laboratory facilities. In general terms, it is possible to distinguish three levels into which monitoring programmes can be classified.

All elements of assessment, from objective setting to data interpretation, are related to these three levels. The aim is to progressively develop monitoring operations from the basic level to the more comprehensive levels. Each level is associated with increasing demands on staff (expertise and numbers), inspection and fieldwork (complexity and frequency), laboratory facilities (range of analysis, throughput) and data management and reporting capacity.

Training of Staffs

The personnel in charge of sample collection, field handling and field measurements must be trained for these activities. The choice of personnel for sampling depends on a number of factors, including the geographic features of the region and the systems for transportation. For example, in a small country with good transport infrastructure, sampling may be carried out by laboratory personnel going to the field to take samples, conduct field analyses and transport samples back to the laboratory.

In countries of a larger size that possess a more developed monitoring system, specially-trained field personnel often conduct the sampling and inspection. In large countries that have a poor transportation system, relatively more personnel are required. In this situation specialists from decentralised facilities, such as health centres or hydrometereological and hydrological stations, may be involved in sampling, inspection and testing. Such personnel may not always possess all appropriate training.

Separate training packages should be developed for field staff, laboratory staff and others. It should be emphasised that training is not a "once-only" activity, but should be continuous. Supervision, as a form of training, is especially relevant to laboratory and field staff. It is vital that the training function is flexible, responding to experience and feedback and taking account of specific needs. Training is especially important when programmes for monitoring are implemented in several countries or independently managed areas or regions, from which the results will be compared and used outside the country or region where the monitoring has taken place.

Assuming a good general education or relevant previous experience, the training period for staff responsible for fieldwork and sampling is about one week, with approximately one additional week of further training as monitoring develops through basic, intermediate to full levels. In order to maintain motivation, it is recommended, that short follow-up events are provided. If the staff are less experienced more training will be necessary.

Although not exhaustive, training for field staff should include the objectives of the water quality monitoring programme and its local, national and international significance. The training should stress the importance of samples being of good quality and representative of the water body from which they are taken and it should give guidance on how to ensure that the samples meet those requirements. The training should also include planning of field sampling and map reading, as well as how to make field notes describing the sampling site and station and how to undertake on-site inspections. Safety aspects of field sampling are an important component of the training programme.

Staffing requirements for servicing a monitoring programme may vary widely and it is not possible to make general statements about the number of staff needed for fieldwork. Estimating staffing requirements includes allowing for travel time or distance between beaches and laboratory, the choice of laboratory infrastructure (e.g. centralised or decentralised) and co-ordination between participating institutions.

The head of the laboratory and/or the programme manager are generally responsible for:

— Laboratory management.
— Determining and procuring the equipment and supplies that will be required.
— Ensuring that Standard Operating Procedures (SOPs) are being followed.

— Ensuring that adequate quality control procedures are being followed.

— Enforcing safety procedures.

Laboratory technicians must have suitable training. They will generally be responsible for:

— Maintenance of the laboratory including, cleanliness and safe storage of all equipment, glassware and other reusables.

— Storage and preparation of reagents and media.

— Checking the accuracy of field equipment.

— Training of junior staff.

— Performing the tests and recording the results of field analyses.

Analytical Facilities

The choice of laboratories to be involved in the monitoring programme can have a major influence on the time required for collecting the samples. There may be reasons such as ensuring staff training, equipment repair and analytical quality control, that suggests using a central laboratory is more appropriate. Nevertheless, when total sample numbers are high and samples are transported over long distances, it may be preferable to use more than one laboratory. Under these circumstances it is normal practice for one of the laboratories to act as the central or co-ordinating laboratory. Some countries have developed mobile laboratories (typically in small vans or minibuses) as an alternative solution to the problems of sample transport. Where long distances are encountered this has often been found to be an effective approach. The need for co-ordination between institutions, for example when sampling is undertaken by one agency and analysis by another, may reduce the necessary workload but may lead to inefficiency if the co-ordination is not effective.

In many countries, monitoring laboratories are organised on two tiers: regional laboratories (lower level) to conduct basic determinations not requiring very complex equipment, and central laboratories (higher level) to conduct more complex analyses requiring elaborate equipment and well trained personnel. In addition, the central laboratories often provide the regional laboratories with methodologies and analytical data quality control.

During the initial stages of development of a recreational water monitoring system, it is reasonable to focus on the basic variables that, as a rule, do not require expensive and sophisticated equipment. Gradually, the number of variables measured can be increased in relation to the financial resources of the monitoring agency. Even in fully-developed monitoring programmes, the elaborate equipment and technical skills necessary for the measurement of complex variables are not needed in every laboratory.

Laboratories must be selected or set up to meet the objectives of each assessment programme. Attention should be paid to the choice of analytical methods. The range of concentrations measured by the chosen methods must correspond to the concentrations of the variable in a water body and to the concentrations set by any applicable water quality standards. Ideally, a laboratory should consist of four sections:

— Reception and registration of samples.

— Production of analytical media.

— Sample analysis.

— Washing up and autoclaving equipment.

Transport and Scheduling

Resource elements in fieldwork include transportation, personnel requirements and equipment. Problems of transport are largely related to distance and accessibility of sampling sites. Where access to sites is known to be problematic, reliance has been placed traditionally on four-wheel drive vehicles, but these are often expensive to purchase and to operate. It may generally be assumed that the main part of the beaches included in the routine monitoring programme can be reached using ordinary vehicles because beaches difficult to access have most probably been excluded when selecting the participating beaches.

Some beaches may be located such that using motorcycles or public transport is a possibility; however, most frequently, ordinary cars equipped for transportation of the samples will be required. Sampling transport equipment can consist of an insulated box with melting ice, or a refrigerator installed in the vehicles, to ensure that the samples are kept cool.

Travel time to and from sampling sites is a major constraint for staff undertaking fieldwork. Realistic estimates of travel time to each sampling site should be made as early in the programme as possible. An inventory of sampling stations should be developed, including actual travelling time, in order to facilitate programme planning. When planning the route for visiting the sites, the demand of having the samples analysed at the laboratory within the appropriate time frame must also be taken into account.

Inspection Programmes

Public health authorities should have, at least, a basic inspection programme in place for all recreational-water sites within their jurisdiction. The primary purpose of the inspection programme is to minimise the risk of illness or accident to bathers. The programme should be based on an SOP. This will ensure that the on-site inspection, laboratory analyses and interpretation of data are carried out in an objective and uniform manner. An on-site survey form should be prepared as a guide for inspectors to make certain that all aspects of the site receive adequate review and evaluation.

In most programmes at least two forms will be used. The first "basic registration" form collects the minimum background information to construct a register. The beach register is a high priority during the basic level of monitoring. The principal uses of the beach register are:

— To determine which beaches should be considered by the programme, based upon criteria such as extent of use, degree of development (or plans to develop) and already-recognised hazards.

— To provide data (such as transport options and travel times) to assist in programme planning.

Once a beach enters into a monitoring programme it will be subject to periodic, usually annual, inspections. These inspections are principally orientated towards the identification of hazards that might lead to physical injury or contribute to drowning; towards the adequacy of measures (signs, lifeguards, communications) in place to reduce these risks; and towards sources of microbiological pollution such as sewage outfalls, combined sewer overflows, rivers and storm drains. At freshwater sites, the inspection may also be concerned with the likelihood of cyanobacterial blooms.

A key requirement of any inspection programme is the availability of qualified personnel. Ideally, inspectors should have a basic knowledge of public health microbiology, environmental chemistry, limnology, oceanography, estuaries and meteorology. Training workshops, based on SOPs and actual case studies, should be held during programme development and implementation. Additional workshops should be held periodically to review inspection procedures.

The co-operation of all involved or interested individuals or organisations is essential if assessments and monitoring programmes are to result in improved water quality and reduced health risks. Representatives from user groups, tourist associations, beach and resort owners, industries and sewage treatment facilities and public health laboratories should be aware of, and invited to participate in, the programme. The complexity and completeness of surveys are likely to increase as programmes develop from local through basic and intermediate to full levels.

At the most advanced level, for each site, three to five days may be required to prepare for the survey, conduct an inspection and prepare the report, although subsequent re-verification visits may require less time. From these findings public health authorities will be able to classify the beaches within their jurisdiction with ratings ranging from excellent to very poor and to relate these ratings to requirements for monitoring and management.

Data Processing and Interpretation

If data have been collected in a careful manner in a properly designed study, they will be representative and unbiased and suitable for analysis, interpretation and reporting. Processing, management and storage of data can be collectively described by the term "data handling". The data handlers receive data from samplers and interviewers in the field, as well as the results of analyses from laboratories. They then assemble and archive the data in central files and analyse the data as instructed, so that they can be interpreted by those responsible for reporting the results. It is most desirable to prevent bias, from the introduction of personal or political perceptions, by arranging for separate groups of people to carry out the collection, handling and interpretation of data.

Data handlers must be appropriately trained and qualified for their duties. It is also desirable that the data handlers do not have any particular interest in the results of the study, apart from carrying out their work with dedication and accuracy. The whole process of the study should be under the control of a study director, who will receive instructions on the objectives and on the programme to be carried out as well as statistical and other scientific advice from appropriate experts. In this way, the requirements for effective data management will be fulfilled. The period over which the data may be needed and the purpose for which they could be used should be considered at the outset, particularly for large or continuing studies.

Computer hardware and software systems inevitably change over time and future compatibility could be a problem. For example, it is doubtful whether data stored on punched cards or paper tape some 30 years ago could now be retrieved. Moreover, changes in methods of analysis will reduce the compatibility of data from older studies with those of recent studies, thus rendering the raw data (but not necessarily the conclusions) less useful. Consideration should be given to storing data in several places, and in more than one format, in order to forestall the risk of loss and damage.

For the long term, it is vital to ensure that published reports carry adequate details of the methods of surveys and that the key data and basic statistics, such as means and standard deviations of measurements, are recorded as appendices to the final reports. The basic test of the adequacy of survey recording is whether an independent investigator could understand what was done sufficiently to be able to repeat the work and to be able to test the results and conclusions from the data presented.

The greatest cost of any study is the data collection. These data will be unique and there will usually be no opportunity of repeating a missing or erroneously recorded observation. The raw data sheets should be examined critically by the person in charge of collecting the data as soon as possible after recording, so that discrepancies can be detected and corrected while the events can still be remembered. It may be possible to check suspect meteorological and tidal records with those obtained at nearby, official recording stations. Different sets of data (e.g. from different sites, sampling runs or days) must not be pooled, unless it has been shown that there is no significant statistical difference between the data sets.

It must be remembered that data are collected for a specific purpose, and thus they may not be useful for meeting subsequent objectives. Most data from routine, regulatory monitoring fall into the "data-rich, information-poor" category because other information, necessary for explaining the circumstances or trends, was not recorded at the time. The use of statistical methods to test a priori null hypotheses is an obligatory part of scientific method. However, the temptation to carry out further analysis of the complete data set at a later date, in order to detect statistically significant associations or correlations between variables, is strictly invalid unless used solely as a method of suggesting hypotheses for further study. Such "data dredging" is analogous to fitting targets to holes.

The effects studied in behavioural and epidemiological research of water recreation are typically small and are difficult to separate from confounding factors (i.e. factors that affect the responses of the exposed and control groups differently). Potentially confounding factors must be identified at the planning stages of a study and suitable measures should be introduced into the design of the study (e.g. by the matching of exposed and non-exposed subjects, or by random assignment) and in the analysis of the data to detect or nullify them.

Confounding can be detected or corrected for in analysis by various methods, such as stratification of the exposed and non-exposed groups (e.g. by common potential confounders such as age, sex or socio-economic class) or by including potential confounders as variables in multivariate analyses, such as logistic regression analyses. It is not possible to eliminate the effects of confounding in the data, if it has not been considered, measured and examined in the design of the study.

Database Construction

The construction of the database will depend on:

— The level of monitoring and the intended use of the data, e.g. for compliance monitoring, risk assessment, baseline data, acquisition, new scheme design, epidemiological investigations and/or post-audit evaluations or remediation efficacy.

— The technology available.

— The requirement for data transfer to regulators or to other agencies.

— The requirements for "data audit" and "chain of evidence" procedures.

There are many data storage systems available that have been developed by laboratories and software engineers.

Perhaps the most stringent and sophisticated database would be characterised by a data storage system able to accommodate the information suitable for a full "chain of evidence" assessment. This type of database is being developed in drinking water surveillance monitoring. The reason for the high level of laboratory audit stems from the potential litigation that could derive from contaminated waters and associated disease outbreaks. This type of database is emerging in drinking water assessment in the UK following a consultation document produced by the Drinking Water Inspectorate.

The requirements of such a data storage programme are that the data could be used in a court of law to achieve a criminal prosecution. To achieve this the prosecution is generally required to demonstrate that the data are accurate beyond reasonable doubt, i.e. the analyst can prove that there are systems in place to prevent tendentious or accidental misreporting through laboratory analytical error or database construction mistakes.

Laboratory audit control is now routine in laboratories undertaking compliance assessment programmes for recreational and drinking waters in some countries. Here, the recording laboratory must be in a position to prove that the recorded value is correct and that laboratory procedures have been followed. The level of internal control is less than for "chain of evidence" assessments, i.e. the laboratory would have to prove that all reasonable measures had been taken but it would not have to demonstrate that there was no error "beyond reasonable doubt".

Any environmental sampling programme should implement appropriate intralaboratory and interlaboratory analytical quality control (AQC) procedures. These would normally involve the collection of field and laboratory blank (e.g. sterile) samples to investigate the integrity of aseptic techniques and field duplicate samples to investigate reproducibility. Generally, it is preferable to use split samples from the same bottle in the case of duplicate enumerations. In inter-laboratory trials duplicate samples are split, or spiked samples are prepared and delivered to participating laboratories for analysis.

There are many commercial data storage software systems available. The developing international standard is a spreadsheet that facilitates storage, rudimentary statistical analyses, graphical representation and data export for external communication and reporting. Spreadsheet packages are commonly used for the storage and recording of recreational water quality data worldwide.

Such systems are appropriate for the user familiar with computation methods and standard package use. They may require adaptation for the lay user or to make them effective tools for clerical staff with a low level of information technology (IT) skills. In such circumstances, the spreadsheet can be modified with a Graphical User Interface (GUI). This facilitates rigid, but user friendly, data access and export, appropriate and tightly controlled analysis and, where appropriate, data cleaning and security. Perhaps the most widely used programming language in the production of a GUI is Visual Basic. This language can be used to design forms and screen menus to control data input, data analysis and reporting, as well as to provide security through the use of passwords. Visual Basic programming requires a competent programmer but the advantages in its use for data security and quality are very significant.

The data storage system should be appropriate to the intended purpose of the storage exercise. If the objective is to demonstrate chain of evidence or a future audit of the data for compliance, a bespoke system will probably need to be constructed to facilitate clerical input, data checking by non-technical staff, data cleaning after extreme values have been flagged, and clearly defined data reporting as defined by legislation. Here, linking a GUI with a spreadsheet through Visual Basic is probably the most appropriate route. Where the data are simply being stored for scientific and/or baseline definition purposes, and no immediate audit beyond normal AQC is required, the spreadsheet alone can be a suitable vehicle for data storage.

Determining Compliance with a Standard

Many monitoring programmes are designed to ascertain compliance with a standard or other objective for water quality. The standard should be carefully checked to determine the method that will be needed to assess compliance. Any deviation from the specified method will lead to doubts about comparability of the conclusions between parallel programmes in different regions, nationally or internationally. The compliance method will have three basic components: the design of the sampling scheme, (including the number of samples, their frequency and the period of sampling); the description of water quality (such as the chemical, physical or microbiological variable), the units of measurement and the descriptive statistics used to describe the level attained in the set of observations (such as the range of values, the average, median, or geometric mean, the standard deviation, or a given percentile value); and the criterion for judging passing or failing of the standard, or for classifying the quality at the water recreation area.

Water quality at a particular site is, essentially, a continuous population of measurements of quality, from which a sampling programme can only provide a limited number of discrete measurements. Because of the errors of measurement that occur when a small number of samples are taken, the sampling programme only gives an approximate estimate of the conditions existing over the whole period of the programme. These errors may, or may not, be regarded as important, although they will have most significance when assessing compliance of waters which are of borderline quality in terms of the standard. Once this problem is recognised, it is important to consider the burden of proof required to assess compliance. It is most usual to take results at their face value, without taking account of sampling error. This is justifiable, but is an empirical decision which will always carry a risk of misclassifying waters, particularly if small numbers of samples are taken. Alternatively, allowance may be made for sampling errors by adopting a "benefit of the doubt" or a fail-safe approach, so that when water quality is borderline the risk of incorrectly failing or passing the standard, respectively, is acceptably small and defined in statistical terms.

Most standards specify a limiting value, which may be either a measure of central tendency, such as a mean or median value obtained over a specified period, or an upper limit which must not be exceeded. An upper limit may be absolute, or it may allow for the natural variability that occurs with time and which is caused by such factors as weather and tidal conditions. Such allowance can be made by defining an upper confidence limit, defined statistically by the observed variability or by the percentage of samples (percentile) which must not exceed the upper limit.

Data Presentation

In all except the smallest surveys, the study director and data handlers will wish to use electronic computation for speed and accuracy. They should, however, use reliable and proven statistical packages and assure themselves that the calculation routines give the correct output. Manual calculation may be the only method available to small teams, handling small data sets and lacking computation facilities, or for field use. It can also be invaluable as a means of checking the data as they are produced, or for checking the output from computation. Desk calculators that provide a printed output of the operations and calculations are recommended because the printout provides a means of checking errors of input.

Graphical methods can be used manually when the data set is small. Linear probability graph paper, which has ordinates ruled in equal divisions and abscissae ruled proportionally to the percentage points of the standard normal density function, can be used to check that the data (transformed if necessary) conform approximately to the normal distribution. If so, the graph paper can then be used to estimate the median, other percentile points and the standard deviation of a set of data, with two-figure accuracy.

Water quality data points may be plotted sequentially on a chart to indicate changes of quality with date of sampling. The occurrence of high values may be used to initiate investigation. In these circumstances the plot becomes a control chart. The choice of a limit value and appropriate action, for when the limit is exceeded, will be chosen to suit the need. The limit value can be set to coincide with the value given in a standard. More conventionally, two upper limit values are set on a control chart: at the mean plus twice and at the mean plus three times the sample standard deviation. These represent values that would be expected to be exceeded only once in 20 or 100 samples and which indicate, respectively, a warning and the need for remedial action.

Use of a computer is obligatory for analysing large sets of data. Even when it is possible to use a hand-held calculator or even to use graphical methods, the computer is able to produce results free from error and, in many cases, to reduce the total time expended in data analysis. There are many statistical packages available that can take raw data from a spreadsheet and subject them to statistical analyses and in many cases use them to produce excellent graphics. Such packages are available to suit different needs.

For general use, typical packages that are commercially available are MINITAB Statistical Software, SAS (Statistical Analysis System), SPSS (Statistical Package for the Social Sciences) and BMD (Bio-Medical Data programs). Specialised computer programs include GENSTAT (a comprehensive collection of statistical programs available from Numerical Algorithms Group Ltd) and EpiInfo (public domain software for epidemiological investigations). Each of these has graphical capabilities adequate for most users, although they can also produce output appropriate for more sophisticated and internationally available graphics and publishing software.

Data Interpretation

Interpretation of data and communication of results are the final two steps in an assessment programme. Correctly interpreted data will not be of much use if they are not disseminated to relevant authorities, to scientists and the public, in a form that is readily understandable by, and acceptable to, the target audience. The form and level of data presentation is, therefore, crucial. Often, it is advisable to produce two types of reports: a comprehensive, detailed report containing all relevant data and associated interpretation and an executive summary (in an illustrated and simple form) which highlights the major findings. Usually, the interpretation of data is undertaken by specialised professionals, such as the relevant scientists, (e.g. microbiologists, chemists or epidemiologists) the data treatment team and professionals from other organisations such as environmental protection agencies, health authorities, national resource agencies.

As a courtesy, the results and recommendations should be discussed with all interested groups and individuals before reports are formally released. A contingency plan should also be developed with the assistance of all those with a vested interest to investigate and respond to cases of adverse health effects or to any unforeseen event or conditions that could lead to a deterioration in water quality and possibly increase the risk of illness to bathers.

A very important part of any sampling exercise is to review the extent to which the desired objectives have been achieved. There are many reasons for periodic adjustments to any assessment or monitoring programme for recreational water quality. The initial objectives may have been achieved and the programme may need reorientating from a baseline study to routine monitoring, with the establishment of new objectives and possibly the addition of supplementary monitoring variables or the substitution of existing activities with new activities. Once the samples have been taken, contemporary information is available on distributions and variability. If the required precision has not been achieved, these new data may be used to establish how many extra samples are required, and how the sampling strategy may be further optimised. If necessary, any extra sampling may then be carried out immediately.

11

Public Participation

Successful tourism management requires an understanding of the nature and dynamics of the destination, i.e. the physical, chemical and biological interactions that take place on and around the destination, the requirements and perceptions of the users, economic and tourism interests and environmental protection measures. Inevitably, there are conflicts between these elements, although many of these conflicts can be resolved through effective communication at an early stage, through information and, above all, active participation of all parties, particularly the public.

The success of tourism management depends very much on the active participation and involvement of the local population and of visitors. The underlying principle is that the public has a right to know, a right to be heard and a right of co-decision. In keeping with the principles of Agenda 21, the public should be involved in information gathering and management of recreational water use areas. In resort areas, the management tasks are usually predominantly in the hands of the local government or health authority.

The public can take an active role in a variety of practical activities concerned with tourism management. The participation of the public in monitoring helps to raise awareness of the condition of the recreational water use area and provides a cost-effective method of gathering large amounts of data which can then be acted upon by tourism managers. Involvement of the public in special interest groups, such as voluntary lifeguard organisations, helps to educate the public for self protection.

Tourism managers have a responsibility to educate the public about hazards related to the recreational water use area, to provide warnings to the public and to provide other information. There are a variety of methods for communicating with the public, such as flags, signs, literature or awards. Whichever method is used, it is imperative that the public understands clearly the message being conveyed.

Public Participation Schemes

A number of community participation schemes have been developed worldwide. An example is the "Officer Snook Program" which was initiated in 1992 at Miami Beach and was sponsored by the United States Coast Guard. This scheme includes videos, slide shows, competitions, cleanups and recycling programmes involving 25,000 elementary schools.

In Glacier Bay, Alaska the prevention of marine debris is an integral part of the visitor management and education programme. Some schemes are aimed at specific types of marine debris. In Tasmania, Australia the use of television advertisements was an integral part of a community awareness programme initiated in response to the growing entanglement of marine mammals and seabirds in marine debris.

In southern Africa, the Dolphin Action and Protection Group launched a national campaign in 1987 entitled "Save our Sealife: Prevent Plastic Pollution". The scheme targeted shipping and fishing companies, industry, schools and the general public, and involved the distribution of pamphlets, the initiation of beach-cleans and the raising of the issue in Parliament. The scheme has now been extended to Antarctica, Namibia and islands in the Southern Atlantic and Indian Oceans.

Education and public awareness are key elements in the reduction of marine debris. Public involvement in tourism management takes two forms: direct action such as cleanups and monitoring; and indirect action, such as education, award schemes and legislation. The involvement of the public in tourism monitoring and cleanup programmes has dual advantages in that it allows a large sample size to be achieved, and raises awareness among society which will then translate into effective individual action to reduce litter at source. Involvement of the public in such campaigns has been achieved world-wide. Coastwatch Europe, for example, involves tens of thousands of volunteers each year in monitoring marine debris.

The largest network organising beach clean events is the Center for Marine Conservation (CMC) based in Washington DC, USA. This centre organises annual beach cleans during "Coastweek" at the end of September and beginning of October. Volunteers use standard recording cards which divide debris into eight major categories according to the fabrication material and a further 65 categories according to type of item. Guidance notes are provided, including an identification guide and information on how the data is used. Volunteers are asked to record the location of the beach and the nearest city, the estimated distance covered and the number of bags filled with debris.

Local Communication

When tourism management plans are operational, further information updates are important. This information needs to involve aspects of safety and quality. Baseline surveys, eco-audits, or shore and hinterland surveys are an excellent way to gather data about the bathing water itself, the surrounding aquatic environment and the hinterland. For resort beaches, the baseline survey should be carried out during the main bathing season, when caravan parks are full, local restaurants are running at peak capacity and facilities such as public toilets and showers are being well used. If a survey is undertaken out of season unexpected events, such as seepage from overloaded septic tanks and storm drains, are likely to be missed. It is essential that the baseline survey is augmented with background information concerning seasonal changes. Such information can be gained from local people, such as year-round swimmers or non-governmental organisations.

Local public participation should be part of the whole exercise from survey to subsequent action. However, it must be borne in mind that involving local public participation during baseline survey data gathering might occasionally invite bias into reporting unless care is taken by the survey team. The baseline survey will provide a variety of information that can be used in plans for informing the beach users and visitors on safety and health risks.

Unless users are aware of the hazards and regulations applicable to particular areas, they are unable to make an informed choice about their destination or to react appropriately to management strategies. While there may be resort areas with an abundance of public information and controls, it is not economically viable, nor necessarily desirable, to extend such infrastructure to rural bathing places, used by only a few people. However, it is in everybody's interest that bathing is as safe as possible even in these isolated areas.

Strategies for accident prevention should first address the removal of hazards. If this is not possible, steps should be taken to reduce the level of risk. Information is particularly important where less can be done physically to reduce the risk. In this regard, all available techniques should be used to convey safety messages, such as the provision of safety signs and notices, flags and brochures.

The primary reason for monitoring bathing water quality and for informing the public is to protect public health. Members of the public are unlikely to want to know the details of sample treatment in the laboratory, although they would need to know whether the water quality is safe. It is essential that information provided to the public is presented in a clear, unambiguous and easily understood way. Some of the cheapest and quickest approaches to assembling and presenting summary data are often the most effective.

Award Schemes

Award schemes are often used as an incentive programme to involve all parties concerned in participating in optimising desitantion safety, quality and education activities. Awards are generally the recognition of effort, or of standard achieved.

Tourism award and evaluation systems are valuable tools for the promotion and management of tourism. Annual and systematic surveys of a variety of parameters, including beach litter, have been undertaken for a number of award schemes. Tourism awards can be important agents for change, integrating a variety of factors, including quality, safety, litter, and management practice in general. Beach resorts, in particular, want these awards and manage their destinations to ensure that they comply with the requirements of the award.

Blue Flag

Probably the most widely known beach award within the European and Mediterranean context is the Blue Flag Award. The Blue Flag scheme is organised by the Federation of Environmental Education in Europe (FEEE). The Blue Flag Campaign was started in 1987 as one of the many activities of the European Year of the Environment. It is a Europe-wide initiative involving more than 1,000 beaches and 500 marinas in 19 European countries. Within the European Union, only "identified" bathing waters within the terms of the Bathing Waters Directive 76/160/EEC are eligible for the award. Outside the European Union, almost any beach could apply for the award via the national operator.

Qualification is based on a wide variety of criteria (some of which are obligatory, others are guideline criteria) divided into four groups: environmental education and information, environmental management, water quality, and safety and services. In terms of the environmental education criteria "the aim of the campaign is to increase the public's environmental awareness and to create a platform for active participation in the protection of the environment".

Co-operation between FEEE and the United Nations Environment Programme, Industry and Environment (UNEP IE) office resulted in a pilot project for implementing the Blue Flag concept in non-European regions. To combine monitoring of Blue Flag holders with gathering extra information, an "In Season Beach Award" was run in Ireland in 1992 for 100 beaches. Points were allocated for a range of criteria and each beach was visited and checked thoroughly by one of a volunteer team.

Costa Rica

Chaverri devised a rating system to identify beaches suitable for governmental and private tourist development in Costa Rica under the authority of the Marine and Terrestrial Act. Up to 113 factors, classed as either positive and negative, were given a score between zero and four, with the final rating score for the beach obtained by subtracting the sum of the "negative" scores from the sum of the "positive" scores. The factors comprised six groups. Some selected factors were water, beach, sand, rock, general beach environment and the surrounding area.

No attempt was made to attribute quantitative values to scores for any of the factors, so that the beach score for any factor was based purely on the subjective judgement of the particular assessor. In addition, no attempt was made to assess the importance attached by beach users to any of the factors in the checklist, to assess which factors were of importance for various types of beaches (apart from a differentiation between sand and rock areas), or to attach weightings to the various factors. Even the rigid division of factors into "positive" and "negative" categories could be considered to be subjective.

Black Sea Environment Programme

The Black Sea Environment Programme aims to strengthen and create regional capacities for managing the Black Sea, in particular by developing policies and legislative frameworks relating to pollution, health, biodiversity, and to attract investment. The programme emphasises the importance of harmonisation of methodologies and standards for evaluation of bathing beaches and beach quality. It provides guidelines for assessment of bathing beaches and bathing water quality, and on how to implement assessment programmes and to evaluate the results.

The programme suggests a questionnaire for registering beach quality that takes into account details concerning beach facilities, physical characteristics of the beach, usage, accessibility, water quality and designation. It does not involve "scoring" the beaches. The final classification is based on the following definition: "a good beach is a safe beach as well as a beach with good water and beach quality". The beach is classified according to any problems discovered and, using this classification, an action programme can be identified. The objective of the programme is then to encourage the use of data to refine the action programmes to solve problems that have been highlighted through the monitoring programmes.

Education

Awareness on safety may be achieved through community education. This can be by means of talks to groups and schools, information sheets and posters, videos or practical activities. Public participation and education can be promoted through government advisory committees, citizens advisory committees, interest group representatives, public hearings, broad dissemination, information gatherings, community meetings, media campaigns, brochures, newsletters, school programmes, community exhibitions and user group training.

School Education

School education differs greatly between countries and also between regions and school types. Most students never see a County Council or Parliament debate and have never asked their local representative to pose a written question for them (such as why the local beach is not designated). In addition, environmental law is rarely taught in schools. Although water quality experiments might be carried out in chemistry and biology classes, and field-work might be undertaken, the results are rarely compared with real data generated by official monitoring programmes.

The involvement of school groups in awareness campaigns such as Coast-watch Europe, in beach cleans such as those organised by the CMC in the USA and in other community participation programmes is becoming more widespread. Understanding provides the ability to make informed decisions. Bathing is practised so widely as a form of recreation that information relating to its safe enjoyment should be widely disseminated beyond swimming classes. A basic understanding of water pollution, water quality and dangers on the shore may be taught beneficially in school such that the knowledge gained is applied early.

Role of Special Interest Groups

Swimming, lifesaving and other local interest groups play an important part in the education and awareness of the public towards recreational water-use quality and safety. Recognition of hazards has led to the introduction of various beach safety regulations and the establishment of lifesaving clubs at many resorts, particularly in the USA, Australia and New Zealand. Surf Life Saving, Australia, for example, is a national organisation co-ordinating 255 Life Saving Clubs and professional lifeguards who patrol 300 beaches and make over 10,000 rescues each year. This organisation has also sponsored the Beach Safety Management Programme, documenting coastal hazards and their impacts on public safety on more than 7,000

Australian ocean beaches. It has developed a database for every beach, showing location, access, nature, physical characteristics, facilities, use, and beach and surf conditions, together with an assessment of risk levels and a prediction of the cost required to maintain adequate levels of public safety on each beach.

12

Sustainable Tourism Management

The concept of sustainability as a resource development and management philosophy is permeating all levels of policy and practice relating to tourism, from local to global. Sustainable tourism management of the natural and physical environment, more than ever before, must coexist with economic, sociocultural, and health and safety objectives of localities and nations. Finding a balance between economic growth and protecting natural resources has challenged rich and poor nations alike to cooperate in sustainable tourism development while otherwise competing for international tourism.

Sustainable tourism development as used in this text means achieving growth in a manner that does not deplete the natural and built environment and preserves the culture of the local community. Within the concept of sustainable tourism development, there is increasing recognition that sustainable management of resources will lead to acceptable conservation and development of a higher quality tourism product. Human beings have control over the use of and modification of the environment in positive (and negative) ways. In brief, tourism can be a tool to enhance the environment or destroy it.

Key elements of tourism sustainability include meeting the needs of visitors and host communities and protecting and enhancing the tourism attraction for the future as part of a national economic resource. The relationship among tourists, host communities, attractions, and the environment is complex and interactive. Each element must maintain its own continuance in symbiosis with the others through development of a mutually beneficial and positive relationship.

The question of funding and obtaining political and policy acceptance of sustainable tourism development can be a major problem area; however, more recently, public and private cooperation is engendering innovative strategies to respond to these concerns. For example, admission charges to natural and historic places can be devised to be commensurate with the uniqueness of the site thereby providing for self-funding of site maintenance and improvements and the moderation of use.

Sensitivity to the environment is rapidly becoming a major component of international tourism marketing strategies; too often we see incidents where visitors become insensitive to their surroundings, suggesting that tourists and the environment may not be entirely compatible. Some tourists want souvenirs such as unusual corals, exotic rocks or colorful sea shells. Others trample irreplaceable tundra or otherwise alter natural flora which can compound the biological damage to other plants and animals. Some people are tempted to chip off a fragment of an Indian abode, steal native artifacts, or otherwise desecrate man-made objects of historic and artistic significance.

The environment in which tourism interacts is broad in scope. It includes not only land, air, water, flora, and fauna but also the man-made changes in the environment including history, culture, and heritage. The tourist must plan for and adapt to societal differences as well, especially when traveling abroad. The environment, in its broad definition, is what attracts many tourists in the first place. Often the greater the mixture of elements in a single trip --- from rain forests to ruins to river rafting --- the deeper and more memorable the experience. In other words, the attraction may be the ecosystem, the wildlife, the rich archeological discoveries, the climate or the culture which the tourist may have read about, or have seen on the television screen. The important message is that whatever the environment may be, it must be nurtured, modified and protected for future generations.

Sustainable Tourism Development

Sustainable tourism development is difficult to define because it must relate today's tourism needs with tomorrow's concern for the future — a difficult task in a dynamic tourism world. The following are the five key elements for tourism sustainability:

1. Preserving the current resource base for future generations.
2. Maintaining the productivity of the resource base.
3. Maintaining biodiversity and avoiding irreversible environmental changes.
4. Ensuring equity within and between generations.
5. Maintaining and protecting the heritage (culture and history) of the area, region, or nation.

The challenge is finding an acceptable balance among these elements. The different business and consumer interests in tourism often overlook the sustainability aspect of tourism. Tourism hosts and guests often see the tourism environment through different glasses.

Eco-efficiency in sustainable tourism development describes those companies and nations taking advantage of the potential success value of incorporating minimum resource use and minimum pollution into public and private sector tourism practices. The New Zealand Ministry of Tourism, for example, provides the following description:

To practice eco-efficiency, tourism developers need to consider the environment creatively, throughout project design, construction and operation. Failure to do so could be costly and cause adverse public attention. Those who are responsible for delivering products and services to the visitor must examine their operations in light of sustainable resource management. This may involve any of the following actions:

— protecting the biosphere

— reducing and disposing of wastes

— adopting energy efficient practices

— minimizing environmental risks

— undertaking "green" marketing

— mitigating environmental marketing

— providing complete and credible environmental information for visitors

— incorporating environmental values in the management of operations

— conducting regular environmental audits

Fortunately, increasing numbers of private/public and non-profit entities are recognizing the value of sustainable tourism development and are cooperating in efforts to set aside specific tracts of land for the protection of the natural and built environment. For example in a recent article "Toward a Greener Globe", there is an interesting discussion of the dependence of tourism on the natural and cultural environment. The article suggests that sustainable tourism development "...is both morally right and good business..." for the world's tourism industry. In brief, the article suggests that much of the world's business community is increasingly in step with sustainable tourism development as it reflects society's desire to protect and preserve environments and cultures for future generations to enjoy because "...our survival depends on a healthy environment."

The world increasingly recognizes that the natural environment is under severe pressure. This recognition has crossed political and philosophical borders, and the concept of sustainability and stewardship for future generations has widespread support. The development of long-term policies, rather than short-term fixes, is essential to guarantee that tourism growth occurs in a socially, economically, and environmentally responsible manner.

A conceptual statement of sustainable tourism development can be found in the Pacific Asia Travel Association's "Code for Environmentally Responsible Tourism" as follows:

> Recognizes the necessity to ensure a sustainable future, meets the needs of the tourism industry today, and does not compromise the ability of this and future generations to consume the environment.

This Code succinctly describes where many countries and businesses would like to be with respect to an environmental ethic for tourism.

Achieving a nation's quality of life through tourism is a sobering challenge. This intellectual transformation will never happen by itself. It will come to pass only as an integral part of a regimented policy and planning process for the development of tourism, driven by a universal understanding of the global environment. Such a policy will be successful only if the business community can earn a profit in its commitment to sustainable tourism development.

Conceptual Approach to Sustainable Tourism

Sustainable tourism policy in today's world is a positive approach that seeks to maintain quality tourism products over a sustained period of time in order to meet the growing domestic and international market for environmental tourism experiences. It suggests that, as applied to tourism development, man has the ability to manipulate and modify certain aspects of the environment for better or worse. It recognizes that, unless careful policy prescriptions and management tools are utilized, tourism can degrade the environment and otherwise damage its use by future generations.

A conceptual approach to sustainable tourism development as set forth by the World Conservation Union includes four major principles:

1. *Ecological sustainability*: Development is compatible with the maintenance of essential ecological processes, biological diversity, and biological resources.

2. *Cultural sustainability*: Development increases people's control over their lives, is compatible with the culture and values of those affected, and maintains and strengthens community identity.

3. *Economic sustainability:* Development is economically efficient and resources are managed so they can support future generations.

4. *Local sustainability*: Development is designed to benefit local communities and sustain profits for local businesses.

For sustainable tourism to be successful, it must be endorsed by the tourism industry, government at all levels, key associations, and interested nonprofit organizations. In 1992, a British group known as Tourism Concern, in coordination with the World Wide Fund for Nature, published a discussion document, "Beyond the Green Horizon: A Discussion Paper on Principles for Sustainable Tourism." Principles outlined in this paper include:

— Using resources in a sustainable manner.
— Reducing over-consumption and waste.
— Maintaining diversity.
— Integrating tourism into planning.
— Supporting local economies.
— Involving local communities.
— Consulting stakeholders and the public.
— Training staff.
— Marketing tourism responsibly.
— Undertaking research.

The key to these principles is that sustainable tourism may have commercial interests for companies and that responsibility for sustainable tourism is a shared public-private venture.

Sustainable Tourism Policy

The policy question often raised is: "Can sustainable tourism be economically viable for private companies and local communities while also being sensitive to environmental, cultural and social needs?" A response, of course, must take into account that tourism sustainability must meet the needs of present visitors while fulfilling the goals of the host community and protecting and enhancing the environmental aspects of the attraction for the future. There is no easy policy to achieve these desirable goals, except that a successful and well-developed tourism program should include sustainable management and seek to meet the economic, ecological, social, cultural, and security objectives of the local community.

Another question raised is that sustainable tourism development cannot meet or will detract from policies aimed at economic growth. Sustainable tourism development policy should not be thought of as anti-growth. In fact, in most circumstances, sustainable tourism development is pro-growth. It has the capacity to increase the quality and lifetime value of the tourism products and, hence, increase visitor satisfaction. Satisfied visitors are often repeat visitors and in the long run are key to the overall growth of tourism to a local community. The more important question to answer is whether governments, private sector entities, local communities, non-profit organizations, and tourists, are ready to accept, plan for, participate in, lobby for, and manage tourism programs which are environmentally, socially, culturally and economically sensitive and necessary for sustainable growth.

Local community efforts to develop or expand tourism should, after appraising its tourism potential, develop a set of policy guidelines for sustainable tourism development. Some guiding principles might include the following three propositions:

— Marketing the environmental aspects of a tourism product enhances the promotional values;

— Well-managed tourism programs support a protected environment, and

— Successful tourism businesses need a high quality environment.

Looking at proposition one, marketing tourism as environmentally sound fosters awareness of the earth's finite resources. Through differences in the built environment and differing cultures, the visitor gets a better understanding of the importance of solidarity with the peoples of the world.

The second proposition suggests that travel must take place so that it helps maintain and protect natural and man-made attractions while allowing wide access to the natural environment and the cultural heritage. Developing new environmentally sound tourism products, recognizing visitor carrying capacities, creating cooperative programs with the private sector are ways in which a local community can better manage sustainability of its tourism attractions.

Turning to the third proposition, tourism businesses today recognize that a quality environment enhances their ability to develop and expand the tourism product. They understand that increasingly tourists are demanding products with a strong environmental content. Local tourism programs, therefore, need to form partnerships to promote the environmental protection policies in their best interest. In brief, local residents and tourists have the right to live and travel in quality environments.

Global Tourism

Tourism is big business. New research by the World Travel and Tourism Council (WTTC) indicates that tourism in 1995 generated direct and indirect employment for approximately 212 million people worldwide, or about one in every nine workers. According to the report, global tourism is a $3.4 trillion industry that will continue to grow in the future. WTTC projections suggest that the tourism industry will be a $7.2 trillion industry by 2005, providing about 338 million jobs. Equally important, is that the tourism industry has recognized that the future of tourism depends on the economic development of tourism in harmony with concerns for the environment and culture.

Another recent report, by the Stanford University Research Institute, predicts worldwide tourism will increase by 8 percent over the next several years. Such growth is more than double the predicted growth of most countries Gross Domestic Product. Interestingly, this same report suggests that adventure and culture-based tourism will increase at an annual rate of 10-15 percent, while nature-based tourism will increase by an extraordinary rate of 25-30 percent.

Furthermore, looking at international tourism only (i.e., excluding the larger component, domestic tourism), there were, according to the World Tourism Organization (WTO), some 567 million international travelers in 1995. Estimated international tourism receipts for this same period were over $371 billion (excluding expenditures of $60 billion for international transport). Just as important is that international tourism has had a healthy growth rate. Over the past 10 years worldwide international tourist arrivals have grown at the average rate of 5.5 percent per year, and, more significantly, international tourism receipts have grown at the average rate of 12.5 percent.

The Americas enjoyed a healthy rise in international tourism and increased their worldwide market share in 1995. International tourist arrivals to the Americas reached approximately 112 million in 1995 with international tourism receipts of over $95 billion. South America has emerged as one of the world's fastest growing tourism regions. Inbound tourism also grew in the Caribbean, with cruises in this region featured as one of the fastest-growing categories of leisure travel.

Local Tourism

What global numbers do not tell us is what is happening across the Americas with respect to the economic benefits of tourism to local communities. There have been many studies conducted regarding the economic, social, cultural and environmental aspects of tourism on local communities. The results, for the most part, are very positive. However, a local community contemplating using tourism as an economic development tool should do so only after conducting a comprehensive study of the community.

Tourism is not necessarily a panacea for resolving all the economic woes of a community. A careful cost/ benefit analysis as well as economic, cultural and environmental impact studies should be conducted. A key consideration in an overall evaluation of the tourism impact is to determine if sustainable tourism development is or will meet the needs of present and future tourists as well as the needs of the host community.

In general, most studies of the impact of tourism on local communities have found that a well-researched, well-planned and well-managed tourism program which takes into account the local, natural and cultural environment has a good chance of improving the local economy and enhancing the quality of life for local residents. Some of the economic benefits include developing new businesses, job growth, increased income, product development, improved infrastructure, and special opportunities to link with other services and products. If approached in the right way, it can also promote community pride and yield a higher quality of life.

Local economic benefits also include the potential for profitable domestic industries - hotels, restaurants, transport systems, souvenirs and handicrafts and guide services. If local tourism attracts large numbers of international visitors it can generate sizable amounts of foreign exchange. Other benefits might include:

— diversifying local economies, particularly in rural areas when agricultural employment may be sporadic or insufficient;

— stimulating the rural economy by creating demand for agricultural produce and injecting capital;

— stimulating improvements to local transportation and communications infrastructure, which brings benefits to local people.

A community should carefully assess its historic sites and buildings, traditions, culture, heritage, attractions and natural beauty. Sustainability of tourism would then suggest preserving these valuable assets for future generations and for long-term economic and social gain. The economic value in the protection of such assets helps both small and large communities enhance the overall tourism potential. Recent studies have demonstrated that an increasing number of travelers are interested in seeing and doing more and are willing to stay longer and spend more money in areas that sustain the culture and environment.

Redefining Sustainable Tourism

The above sections have attempted to bring into focus the economic aspects of sustainable tourism development.

This economic definition of sustainable tourism development has focused on optimal management of the tourism environment. It seeks the benefits of economic development, subject to maintaining the services and quality of the natural and built environment for tourists. Part of this economic concept is that if we preserve and conserve the tourism environment today, we can sell our tourism product not only today but also in the future.

This strategy assures future generations of not only a quality environment but also a way to maintain and possibly improve their living standards. It suggests that economic growth through tourism can be compatible with sustainable tourism development, in other words, quality growth. It also strongly indicates that tourism development must be participatory and must involve local peoples and businesses in decisions that affect their lives. Reaching the goal of sustainable tourism development requires simultaneous progress along at least five dimensions -- economic, human, environmental, political, and technological. There are close links among these different dimensions, and actions in one area can reinforce, expand, or enhance goals in another.

Sustainable tourism development may require some changes in existing policies and practices depending on each locale. Some of the changes may be major, but the results will be worth it in the long run. Progress will depend on strong leadership and the continued efforts of people in local communities across the globe. Increasingly, this will include a growing body of private organizations interested and dedicated to positive influences in the direction of environment and development policies around the world. For the most part, they believe that local participation and/or control is the key to the basis of sustainable tourism development.

Sustainable Tourism: Key to Economic Growth

By now it is clear that sustainable tourism can aid economic growth and should be embraced in any economic development process for tourism. Tourist attractions in both the natural and built environments are tremendous engines for economic growth. Such attractions as unspoiled natural ecosystems, well-maintained historic sites and cultural heritage events produce economic gains and quality of life benefits.

The problem that governments and the private sector often have with defining the economics of protecting the environment is attempting to assign values to the protected resource. Measures are in the process of being developed but as yet are not easily defined. Some economic research is ongoing to produce environmental indicators along the same line as economic indicators. The key will be finding good management techniques to support sustainable tourism goals.

Guidelines for Sustainable Tourism Development

The key to sustainable tourism development is to manage the environment (natural, man-made, and cultural) effectively to provide benefits to local people and to enhance the interest of visitors. Customs and traditions must not be discarded and privacy and dignity must be maintained.

When guidelines are contemplated, there are certain basic precepts to keep in mind:

— The first requisite is to inventory, assess and develop as many visitor attractions as possible with roots in the local community or complement local activities. Local culture and heritage, if properly developed, can improve the overall ambiance of the area and also add to the quality of community life. At the same time, local pride and cleanliness of the area may evolve as tourism moves throughout the community.

— Development within each local community should strive to keep the uniqueness of the environment preserved. If there are period historical buildings, special natural resources, or sensitive culture traits available, capitalize on these and let further development or restoration take these aspects into account. This approach keeps the authenticity of the area intact which enriches its value to the visitors and local people alike.

— It is not possible to develop realistic guidelines for sustainable tourism development without community involvement. Not only is it good public relations to encompass the local population in the tourism development process, but it will also result in the ultimate success of the endeavor. The community then becomes an effective force in assisting in the implementation of the program.

— A local community should seek to measure tourism development in light of environmental and social costs and benefits to the community. Sustainable tourism should be viewed in terms of both short term and long term value to the community. Intangible values such as "quality of life" should be added or included in the overall quantification of sustainable tourism development.

Rural Areas

Many rural areas of the world are looking for alternative economic development to replace the former reliance on agricultural and mining products. As agriculture becomes more mechanized and mineral resources more scarce, economic planners are looking for new industries. Many areas are looking towards more sustainable resources as a development tool. Tourism is a highly viable option because its implementation relies on an area's cultural, historic, ethnic, geographic, and natural uniqueness. Such changes are increasingly being viewed as opportunities for keeping rural communities economically viable.

In its 1991-1992 report on tourism, the Organization for Economic Cooperation and Development (OECD) states that the question of suitability of rural areas for tourism development involve six factors:

— Scenic value - including mountains, seashores, lakes islands, rivers, and special interest scenery such as wetlands or mixed deciduous forest;
— Special wildlife assets;
— Cultural assets including historic buildings, towns, villages, sites, and/or ethnic heritage of all types;
— Special facilities for sports including hunting, fishing, skiing, hiking, etc.;
— Ease of access by large populations;
— Effective promotional, commercial, and management skills.

The OECD adds that these factors are not exclusive, and that the possession of any one or all of these factors does not necessarily guarantee success. Yet the consideration of these questions and factors can help potential interests determine if their development ideas and resources at hand warrant further planning effort.

Often rural populations living close to areas that can be utilized for sustainable tourism development are characterized by very low incomes, with few viable economic options. Sustainable tourism can represent for these people a valid economic alternative with the additional advantage that these inhabitants can be converted into conservationists of their natural areas since their welfare depends on the protection of their natural environment. Because of their knowledge of the area, its history, and culture, local residents have the potential to be trained as guides, to work in other local tourism services including accommodations and restaurants, or to own their own tourism-related businesses.

Principles of Sustainable Tourism

Sustainable tourism development can fulfill economic, social, and aesthetic needs while maintaining cultural integrity and ecological processes. It can provide for today's hosts and guests while protecting and enhancing the same opportunity for the future. That's the good news. But sustainable tourism development also involves making hard political choices based on complex social, economic, and environmental trade-offs. It requires a vision which encompasses a larger time and space context than that traditionally used in community planning and decision making. The local planner can use the following principles as basic guidelines when attempting to incorporate this broader vision into local policies and practices.

— Tourism planning, development and operation should be part of conservation or sustainable development strategies for a region, a province (state) or the nation. Tourism planning, development and operation should be cross-sectoral and integrated, involving different government agencies, private corporations, citizens groups and individuals thus providing the widest possible benefits.

— Agencies, corporations, groups and individuals should follow ethical and other principles which respect the culture and environment of the host area, the economy and traditional way of life, the community and traditional behavior, leadership and political patterns.

— Tourism should be planned and managed in a sustainable manner, with due regard for the protection and appropriate economic uses of the natural and human environment in host areas.

— Tourism should be undertaken with equity in mind to distribute fairly benefits and costs among tourism promoters and host peoples and areas.

— Good information, research and communication on the nature of tourism and its effects on the human and cultural environment should be available prior to and during development, especially for the local people, so that they can participate in and influence the direction of development and its effects as much as possible, in the individual and the collective interest.

— Local people should be encouraged and expected to undertake leadership roles in planning and development with the assistance of government, business, financial and other interests.

— Integrated environmental, social, and economic planning analyses should be undertaken prior to the commencement of any major projects, with careful consideration given to different types of tourism development and the ways in which they might link with existing uses, ways of life and environmental considerations.

— Throughout all stages of tourism development and operation, a careful assessment, monitoring and mediation program should be conducted in order to allow local people and others to take advantage of opportunities or to respond to changes.

Guidelines for Nature Tourism

Nature tourism is of growing importance to those countries and regions interested in sustainable tourism. It is one segment of the industry which is difficult to define because it covers a wide range of activities. Nature tourists can be people casually walking through an undisturbed forest, or scuba divers admiring coral formations, or bird watchers adding birds to their lists. But, it is a segment of the market that will respond to environmental issues. The following guidelines can be used by the local planner to encourage community, environmental, and tourism constituencies to work together toward a common goal.

— The success of nature tourism depends on the conservation of nature. Many parks are threatened, and it is critical for everyone involved with nature tourism to realize that intact natural resources are the foundation.

— Nature tourism sites need revenue for protection and maintenance, much of which can be generated directly from entry fees and sales of products. Many protected areas charge nominal or no entrance fees and provide few if any auxiliary services. Nature tourists also desire gift shops, food services and lodging facilities and expect to pay for them.

— Tourists are a valuable audience for environmental education. In many parks, opportunities are missed to provide environmental education. Whether "hard-core" nature tourists or "new" visitors with little background in natural history, all tourists can enhance their appreciation of the area through information brochures, exhibits and guides.

— Nature tourism will contribute to rural development when local residents are brought into the planning process. For nature tourism to be a tool for conservation and rural development, a concerted effort must be made to incorporate local populations into development of the tourism industry. In some cases, tourism to protect areas is not benefiting the surrounding population because they are not involved.

— Opportunities are emerging for new relationships between conservationists and tour operators. Traditionally, these groups have not worked together; often they have been in direct opposition. However, as more tourists come to parks and reserves, tour operators have the opportunity to become more actively involved with the conservation of these areas through education for their clientele and donations to park management.

Charter of Sustainable Tourism

(Developed at the World Conference on Sustainable Tourism, in Lanzarote, Canary Islands, Spain on 27-28 April 1995.)

We, the participants at the World Conference on Sustainable Tourism, meeting in Lanzarote, Canary Islands, Spain, on 27-28 April 1995,

Mindful that tourism, as a worldwide phenomenon, touches the highest and deepest aspirations of all people and is also an important element of socioeconomic and political development in many countries.

Recognizing that tourism is ambivalent, since it can contribute positively to socio- economic and cultural achievement, while at the same time it can contribute to the degradation of the environment and the loss of local identity, and should therefore be approached with a global methodology.

Mindful that the resources on which tourism is based are fragile and that there is a growing demand for improved environmental quality.

Recognizing that tourism affords the opportunity to travel and to know other cultures, and that the development of tourism can help promote closer ties and peace among peoples, creating a conscience that is respectful of the diversity of culture and life styles.

Recalling the Universal Declaration of Human Rights, adopted by the General Assembly of United Nations, and the various United Nations declarations and regional conventions on tourism, the environment, the conservation of cultural heritage and on sustainable development.

Guided by the principles set forth in the Rio Declaration on the Environment and Development and the recommendations arising from Agenda 21.

Recalling previous declarations on tourism, such as the Manila Declaration on World Tourism, the Hague Declaration and the Tourism Bill of Rights and Tourist Code.

Recognizing the need to develop a tourism that meets economic expectations and environmental requirements, and respects not only the social and physical structure of destinations, but also the local population.

Considering it a priority to protect and reinforce the human dignity of both local communities and tourists.

Mindful of the need to establish effective alliances among the principal actors in the field of tourism so as to fulfil the hope of a tourism that is more responsible towards our common heritage.

Appeal to the international community and, in particular,

Urge governments, other public authorities, decisionmakers and professionals in the field of tourism, public and private associations and institutions whose activities are related to tourism, and tourists themselves, to adopt the principles and objectives of the Declaration that follows:

1. Tourism development shall be based on criteria of sustainability, which means that it must be ecologically bearable in the long term, as well as economically viable, and ethically and socially equitable for local communities. Sustainable development is a guided process which envisages global management of resources so as to ensure their viability, thus enabling our natural and cultural capital, including protected areas, to be preserved. As a powerful instrument of development, tourism can and should participate actively in the sustainable development strategy. A requirement of sound management of tourism is that the sustainability of the resources on which it depends must be guaranteed.

2. Tourism should contribute to sustainable development and be integrated with the natural, cultural and human environment; it must respect the fragile balances that characterize many tourist destinations, in particular small islands and environmentally sensitive areas. Tourism should ensure an acceptable evolution as regards its influence on natural resources, biodiversity and the capacity for assimilation of any impacts and residues produced.

3. Tourism must consider its effects on the cultural heritage and traditional elements, activities and dynamics of each local community. Recognition of these local factors and support for the identity, culture and interests of the local community must at all times play a central role in the formulation of tourism strategies, particularly in developing countries.

4. The active contribution of tourism to sustainable development necessarily presupposes the solidarity, mutual respect and participation of all the actors, both

public and private, implicated in the process, and must be based on efficient cooperation mechanisms at all levels: local, national, regional and international.

5 . The conservation, protection and appreciation of the worth of the natural and cultural heritage afford a privileged area for cooperation. This approach implies that all those responsible must take upon themselves a true challenge, that of cultural, technological and professional innovation, and must also undertake a major effort to create and implement integrated planning and management instruments.

6 . Quality criteria both for the preservation of the tourist destination and for the capacity to satisfy tourists, determined jointly with local communities and informed by the principles of sustainable development, should represent priority objectives in the formulation of tourism strategies and projects.

7 . To participate in sustainable development, tourism must be based on the diversity of opportunities offered by the local economy. It should be fully integrated into and contribute positively to local economic development.

8. All options for tourism development must serve effectively to improve the quality of life of all people and must influence the so- cio-cultural enrichment of each destination.

9 . Governments and the competent authorities, with the participation of NGOs and local communities, shall undertake actions aimed at integrating the planning of tourism as a contribution to sustainable development.

10. In recognition of economic and social cohesion among the peoples of the world as a fundamental principle of sustainable development, it is urgent that measures be promoted to permit a more equitable distribution of the

benefits and burdens of tourism. This implies a change of consumption patterns and the introduction of pricing methods which allow environmental costs to be internalised. Governments and multilateral organizations should prioritize and strengthen direct and indirected aid to tourism projects which contribute to improving the quality of the environment. Within this context, it is necessary to explore thoroughly the application of internationally harmonised economic, legal and fiscal instruments to ensure the sustainable use of resources in tourism.

11. Environmentally and culturally vulnerable spaces, both now and in the future, shall be given special priority in the matter of technical cooperation and financial aid for sustainable tourism development. Similarly, special treatment should be given to zones that have been degraded by obsolete and high impact tourism models.

12. The promotion of alternative forms of tourism that are compatible with the principles of sustainable development, together with the encouragement of diversification represent a guarantee of stability in the medium and the long term. In this respect there is a need, for many small islands and environmentally sensitive areas in particular, to actively pursue and strengthen regional cooperation.

13. Governments, industry, authorities, and tourism-related NGOs should promote and participate in the creation of open networks for research, dissemination of information and transfer of appropriate knowledge on tourism and environmentally sustainable tourism technologies.

14. The establishment of a sustainable tourism policy necessarily requires the support and promotion of environmentally-compatible tourism management

systems, feasibility studies for the transformation of the sector, as well as the implementation of demonstration projects and the development of international cooperation programmes.

15. The travel industry, together with bodies and NGOs whose activities are related to tourism, shall draw up specific frameworks for positive and preventive actions to secure sustainable tourism development and establish programmes to support the implementation of such practices. They shall monitor achievements, report on results and exchange their experiences.
16. Particular attention should be paid to the role and the environmental repercussions of transport in tourism, and to the development of economic instruments designed to reduce the use of non-renewable
17. The adoption and implementation of codes of conduct conducive to sustainability by the principal actors involved in tourism, particularly industry, are fundamental if tourism is to be sustainable. Such codes can be effective instruments for the development of responsible tourism activities.
18. All necessary measures should be implemented in order to inform and promote awareness among all parties involved in the tourism industry, at local, national, regional and international level, with regard to the contents and objectives of the Lanzarote Conference.

Final Resolution

The World Conference on Sustainable Tourism considers it vital to make the following public statements:

1. The Conference recommends State and regional governments to draw up urgently plans of action for

sustainable development applied to tourism, in consonance with the principles set out in this Charter.

2. The Conference agrees to refer the Charter for Sustainable Tourism to the Secretary- General of the United Nations, so that it may be taken up by the bodies and agen- cies of the United Nations system, as well as by international organizations which have cooperation agreements with the United Nations, for submission to the General Assembly.

The Berlin Declaration on Biological Diversity and Sustainable Tourism

(*International Conference of Environment Ministers on Biodiversity and Tourism 6-8 March, 1997, Berlin*)

We, Ministers and Heads of Delegation, assembled in Berlin for the International Conference on Biodiversity and Tourism from 6 to 8 March, 1997.

Aware that tourism is an important source of economic wealth and one of the fastest growing sectors in the world economy;

Considering that tourism is a world-wide phenomenon involving a growing number of people undertaking more long-distance journeys;

Recognizing that a healthy environment and beautiful landscapes constitute the basis of long-term viable development of all tourism activities;

Observing that tourism increasingly turns to areas where nature is in a relatively undisturbed state so that a substantial number of the world's remaining natural areas are being developed for tourism activities;

Concerned that while tourism may importantly contribute to socio-economic development and cultural exchange, it has, at the same time, the potential for degrading the natural environment, social structures and cultural heritage;

Taking into account that sustainable forms of tourism generate income also for local communities, including indigenous communities, and that their interests and culture require particular attention;

Recognizing also that tourism may generate or increase a demand for wild animals, plants or products made thereof for souvenirs, and thus endanger species and affect protection measures;

Further recognizing that there is a need to value and protect nature and biological diversity as an essential basis for sustainable development;

Convinced that nature has an intrinsic value which calls for the conservation of species, genetic and ecosystem diversity to ensure the maintenance of essential life support systems;

Furthermore convinced that sustainable forms of tourism have the potential to contribute to the conservation of biological diversity outside and inside protected areas;

Bearing in mind that vulnerable areas, including small islands, coasts, mountains, wetlands, grasslands and other terrestrial and marine ecosystems and habitats of outstanding beauty and rich biological diversity, deserve special measures of protection;

Convinced that achieving sustainable forms of tourism is the responsibility of all stakeholders involved, including government at all levels, international organizations, the private sector, environmental groups and citizens both in tourism destination countries and countries of origin;

Determined to work together with all who are involved in the elaboration of international guidelines or rules that harmonize the interests of nature conservation and tourism, that lead towards sustainable development of tourism, and, thus, contribute to the implementation of the Convention on Biological Diversity and the objectives of Agenda 21;

Agree on the following Priciples:

General

1. Tourism activities should be environmentally, economically, socially and culturally sustainable. Development and management of tourism activities should be guided by the objectives, principles and commitments laid down in the Convention on Biological Diversity.
2. Tourism activities which directly or indirectly contribute to the conservation of nature and biological diversity and which benefit local communities should be promoted by all stakeholders.
3. To conserve nature and biological diversity as a major resource of tourism activities, all necessary measures should be taken to ensure that the integrity of ecosystems and habitats is always respected. Additional burdens from tourism development should be avoided in areas where nature is already under pressure from tourism activities. Preference should be given to the modernization and renovation of existing tourism facilities.
4. Measures inspired by the principle of precautionary action should be taken to prevent and minimize damage caused by tourism to biological diversity. Such measures should include monitoring of existing activities and assessment of environmental impacts of proposed new activities, including the monitoring of the negative effects of wildlife viewing.

5. Tourism activities which use environmentally sound technologies for saving water and energy, prevent pollution, treat waste water, avoid the production of solid waste and encourage recycling should be promoted to the fullest extent.

6. Similarly, tourism activities which encourage the use of public and non-motorised transport should be supported wherever possible.

7. All stakeholders including governments, international organizations, the private sector and environmental groups should recognize their common responsibilities to achieve sustainable forms of tourism.

8. Policies and, where appropriate, legislation, environmental economic instruments and incentives should be developed to ensure that tourism activities meet the needs of nature and biological diversity conservation, including mobilizing funding from tourism

9. The private sector should be encouraged to develop and apply guidelines and codes of conduct for sustainable tourism.

10. All stakeholders should cooperate locally, nationally and internationally to achieve a common understanding on the requirements of sustainable tourism. Particular attention should be given to trans boundary areas and areas of international importance.

11. Concepts and criteria of sustainable tourism should be developed and incorporated in education and training programs for tourism professionals. The general public should be informed and educated about the benefits of protecting nature and conserving biodiversity through sustainable forms of tourism. Results of research and concepts of sustainable tourism should be increasingly disseminated and implemented.

Specific

1. Inventories of tourism activities and attractions should be developed, taking into account the impacts on ecosystems and biological diversity. Coordinated efforts of governments, the private sector and all other stakeholders should be undertaken to agree on criteria to measure and assess the impacts of tourism on nature and biological diversity. In this regard, technical and scientific cooperation should be established through the clearing house mechanism of the Convention on Biodiversity.
2. Tourism activities, including tourism planning, measures to provide tourism infrastructure, and tourism operations, which are likely to have significant impacts on nature and biological diversity should be subject to prior environmental impact assessments.
3. Tourism activities should be planned at the appropriate levels with a view to integrate socio-economic, cultural and environmental considerations at all levels. Development, environment, and tourism planning should be integrated processes. All efforts should be made to ensure that integrated tourism plans are implemented and enforced.
4. Tourism should be based on environmentally friendly concepts and modes of transport. Negative impacts of transport on the environment should be reduced, paying particular attention to environmental impacts of road and air traffic, specifically in ecologically sensitive areas.
5. Sports and outdoor activities, including recreational hunting and fishing, particularly in ecologically sensitive areas, should be managed in a way that they fulfill the requirements of nature and biological diversity conservation and comply with the existing

regulations on conservation and sustainable use of species.

6. Special care should be taken that living animals and plants, and products made thereof for souvenirs, are offered for sale only on the basis of a sustainable and environmentally sound use of the natural resources and in conformity with national legislation and international agreements.

7. Whenever possible and appropriate, economic instruments and incentives including awarding of prizes, certificates and eco-labels for sustainable tourism should be used to encourage the private sector to meet its responsibilities for achieving sustainable tourism. The abolition of economic incentives encouraging environmentally unfriendly activities should be strived for.

8. Tourism should be developed in a way so that it benefits the local communities, strengthens the local economy, employs local workforce and wherever ecologically sustainable, uses local materials, local agricultural products and traditional skills. Mechanisms, including policies and legislation should be introduced to ensure the flow of benefits to local communities.

   Tourism activities should respect the ecological characteristics and capacity of the local environment in which they take place. All efforts should be made to respect traditional lifestyles and cultures.

9. Tourism should be restricted, and where necessary prevented, in ecologically and culturally sensitive areas. All forms of mass tourism should be avoided in those areas. Where existing tourism activities exceed the carrying capacity, all efforts should be made to reduce negative impacts from tourism activities and to take measures to restore the degraded environment.

10. Tourism in protected areas should be managed in order to ensure that the objectives of the protected area regimes are achieved. Wherever tourism activities may contribute to the achievement of conservation objectives in protected areas, such activities should be encouraged and promoted, also as cases to test in a controlled manner the impact of tourism on biodiversity. In highly vulnerable areas, nature reserves and all other protected areas requiring strict protection, tourism activities should be limited to a bearable minimum.
11. In coastal areas all necessary measures should be taken to ensure sustainable forms of tourism, taking into account the principles of integrated coastal area management. Particular attention should be paid to the conservation of vulnerable zones, such as small islands, coral reefs, coastal waters, mangroves, coastal wetlands, beaches and dunes.
12. Tourism in mountain areas should also be managed in environmentally appropriate ways. Tourism in sensitive mountain regions should be regulated so that the biological diversity of these areas can be preserved.
13. In all areas where nature is particularly diverse, vulnerable and attractive, all efforts should be made to meet the requirements of nature protection and biological diversity conservation. Particular attention should be paid to the conservation needs in forest areas, grasslands, fresh water eco-systems, areas of spectacular beauty, arctic and antarctic eco-systems.
14. The Ministers gathered in Berlin on 7 and 8 March, 1997, for the International Conference on Biodiversity and Tourism

    — Recommend that the Conference of the Parties to the Convention on Biological Diversity draw up in consultation with stakeholders guidelines or rules for sustainable tourism development on a global level on the basis of the "Berlin Declaration" in order to contribute to the implementation of the Convention's objectives,

— Agree to submit the "Berlin Declaration" to all Parties and Signatory States with the objective of bringing about a discussion at the 4th Conference of the Parties in Bratislava,

— Call upon the Special Session of the General Assembly of the United Nations to support this initiative under the Biodiversity Convention and recommend to the UN General Assembly Special Session to include the subject of sustainable tourism in the future work program of the Commission on Sustainable Development in order to draw increased attention to the objectives of Agenda 21,

— Call on the bilateral and multilateral funding organizations to take into account the principles and guidelines of the "Berlin Declaration" when supporting projects relating to tourism.

Agreed at Berlin, on the 8th of March, 1997.

Bibliography

Archer, B, "Economic Impact Analysis". *Annals of Tourism Research*, 23(3):704-707, 1996.

Bushnell, R. and Hyle, M., *Computerized models for assessing the economic impact of recreation and tourism*, 1985.

Bull, Adrian., *The economics of travel and tourism*. Melbourne, Australia: Longman, 1995.

Eadington, W. R., & Redman, M., "Economics and tourism", *Annals of Tourism Research*, 18: 41-56, 1991.

English, Donald B.K., Bergstrom, John C., "The conceptual links between recreation site development and regional economic impacts". *Journal of Regional Science*, 34(4): 599-611, 1994.

Elkin, R. and Roberts, R., *Evaluating the human resource (employment) requirements and impacts of tourism developments*, 1987.

Fleming, W. R. & Toepper, L., "Economic impact studies: Relating the positive and negative impacts to tourism development", *Journal of Travel Research*. (Summer): 35-42, 1990.

Fletcher, J. E., "Input-output analysis and tourism impact studies", *Annals of Tourism Research*, 16: 514-529, 1989.

Frechtling, D. C., *Assessing the impacts of travel and tourism — Introduction to travel impact estimation*, 1987.

Fox, K. A., *Urban-regional economics, social system accounts, and eco-behavioral science: selected writings*. Ames, IA : Iowa State University Press, 1994.

Lundberg, Donald E., Krishnamoorthy, M. and Stavenga, Mink H., *Tourism Economics.* New York: John Wiley, 1995.

Pleeter, Saul, Economic impact analysis: Methodology and applications. Boston: Maritinus Nijhoff Publishing, 1980.

Richardson, H.W., *Input-output and regional economics.* New York: John Wiley, 1972.

Walsh, R. G., *Recreation Economic Decisions: Comparing Benefits and Costs.* State College, PA. : Venture Publishing, Inc, 1986.

Index